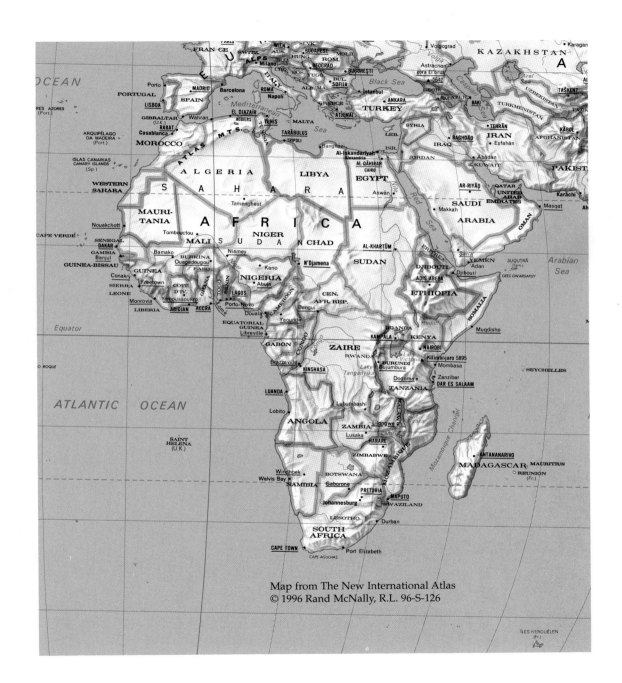

Map from The New International Atlas
© 1996 Rand McNally, R.L. 96-S-126

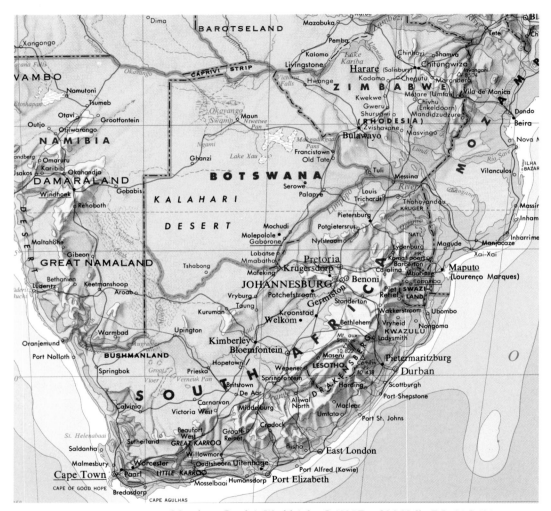

Map from Goode's World Atlas © 1996 Rand McNally, R.L. 96-S-126

Enchantment of the World

SWAZILAND

By Ettagale Blauer and Jason Lauré

Consultant for Swaziland: Lesego Malepe, Ph.D., Assistant Professor of Political Science, Wheaton College, Norton, Massachusetts

CHILDREN'S PRESS®
A Division of Grolier Publishing
New York • London • Hong Kong • Sydney
Danbury, Connecticut

This land is farmed by several families that live near Buckham.

Project Editor and Design:
Jean Blashfield Black
Photo Research: Jay Mallin

Library of Congress
Cataloging-in-Publication Data

Blauer, Ettagale.
    Swaziland / by Ettagale Blauer and
Jason Lauré.
    p. cm. -- (Enchantment of the world)
    Includes index.
    Summary: An overview of a small land-
locked neighbor of South Africa.
    ISBN 0-516-20020-8
    1. Swaziland--Juvenile literature. [1.
Swaziland.] I. Lauré, Jason. II. Title. III.
Series.
DT2719.B55   1996
968.87--dc20   96-2024
                                      CIP
                                      AC

PHOTO CREDITS ©: Tony Stone Images
/Brian Seed: cover; Anthony Bannister Photo
Library /Jody Denham: pp. 4, 8, 71, 81; Lauré
Communications /Steve Hall: pp. 5, 15, 19,
46, 49, 51, 53, 54, 55, 57, 58, 59, 109; TRIP: pp.
6 top (Peter Robinson), 78 (D. Saunders), 107
(S. Harris); Lauré Communications /Jason
Lauré: pp. 6 bottom, 9, 11, 18, 20, 36, 62 top,
64, 67, 72, 73, 74, 76, 80 left, 82, 83, 87 left, 88,
89, 91, 92, 94 top, 94 bottom left, 96, 98, 99,
101 bottom, 102, 103, 108, 111; TRIP /J. Turco;
pp. 10, 62 bottom, 65, 68, 80 right, 85 right,
105; Superstock, Inc.: p. 12; Museum Africa:
pp. 14, 23, 25, 26, 27, 31, 35; National Museum
of African Art; p. 17; North Wind Picture
Archives: p. 22; Bettmann Archive: p. 28;
Bridgeman Art Library: p. 30 (painting by
Spion Kop); AP/Wide World Photos: pp. 34,
41, 44; UPI/Bettmann: pp. 38, 39, 85 left;
Archive Photos: p. 40; United Nations: p. 42;
Anthony Bannister Photo Library: pp. 61
(Robbie Mattner), 87 right (Jason Lauré), 94
bottom right (John Doulton), 101 top (Jason
Lauré).

Map: George Stewart

Cover Photo: A village garden in Swaziland

The red feathers of the colorful bird called a lourie worn by this young woman indicate that she is a member of the royal family.

TABLE OF CONTENTS

The scene above is near Piggs Peak in the mountainous western region of Swaziland. Most of these mountains were once forested, but the trees have been cut for firewood. The sunset-filled valley below is near Manzini, the agricultural center of the country, in the region called the **umphakatsi**, *meaning "headquarters."*

Chapter 1

NATURAL SETTING

The Kingdom of Swaziland is a small, landlocked country located in the southern part of Africa. It is almost encircled by the country of South Africa, which forms its northern, southern, and western borders. On the eastern border lies the country of Mozambique.

Swaziland measures about 120 miles (193 kilometers) from north to south and 90 miles (145 kilometers) from east to west. Within its 6,704 square miles (17,364 square kilometers) are found four physically distinct terrains. Although the country is slightly smaller than the state of Massachusetts, its geography ranges from dramatic mountain ranges to low-lying farmland. Both the land and the climate vary greatly from one region to the next, each section occupying a "belt" that stretches from north to south.

The westernmost belt is a region of mountain ranges, a continuation of the Drakensbergs in neighboring South Africa. These mountains stand 3,500 to 4,500 feet high (1,067 to 1,372 meters), with two of the peaks measuring more than 6,000 feet (1,829 meters). The Swazis call this region *inkhangala,* which means a "cold, treeless place." Despite its name, this high belt is actually very green and covered with foliage in its valleys and deep gorges. This is the coolest part of the country, especially in the higher elevations. It often gets rain even when the rest of the

The middle belt of vegetation is lower and drier than the mountainous region. The major towns of Swaziland are located in this more hospitable part of the country.

country remains dry. Up to 100 inches (254 centimeters) of rain fall in the inkhangala each year.

To the east lies the next belt, just 29 miles (47 kilometers) wide, known as *umphakatsi,* which means "headquarters" in the Swazi language. This is the spiritual homeland of the Swazi people. The elevation here drops down to an average of 2,000 to 2,500 feet (610 to 762 meters). The climate is subtropical, markedly drier and hotter than the mountain belt. The hills are more rounded and are marked by valleys that are riddled with rivers. The region forms the heart of the nation's farmland and has the highest concentration of people in the country.

The aloe plant shown at left is one of many such succulent plants that thrive in the flatter, drier lihlanze, or third "belt." The three main belts, plus the escarpment, that make up Swaziland are shown in the map.

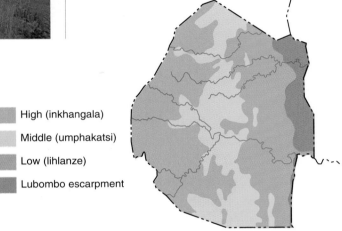

High (inkhangala)

Middle (umphakatsi)

Low (lihlanze)

Lubombo escarpment

Farther to the east is the *lihlanze,* which means a "dry place with trees." This low belt ranges from 500 to 1,000 feet (152 to 305 meters) above sea level. It is the driest and hottest part of the country. Its flat, rolling plains are spotted with thornbush and scrub vegetation.

The fourth region of Swaziland is the Lubombo escarpment, a steep slope that separates the country from Mozambique. This natural barrier rises sharply at the border between the two countries. The climate and elevation here are similar to the umphakatsi, making the region suitable for cattle ranching and small-scale farming.

The Lusutfu River is one of the many rivers used to irrigate farmland. However, the soil often erodes into the water, harming both the land and the river.

RIVERS

Swaziland is well marked by rivers, the most important being the Komati, Lomati, Great Usutu, and Little Usutu. These rivers flow eastward into Mozambique, eventually emptying into the Indian Ocean. They make deep gorges in the Lubombo escarpment. Many smaller rivers also flow throughout the country, allowing for farming by irrigation in many areas.

ANIMALS

The large mammals for which Africa is famous have virtually disappeared from Swaziland. They were victims of overhunting, both legal and illegal, as well as several terrible epidemics of a disease called rinderpest. Most of the larger animals remaining can be seen only in the several nature preserves developed by people who are trying to protect the animals. Giraffes, wildebeests, zebras, hippopotamuses, and several other kinds of antelopes are the main residents. Ostriches, once common on the plains of southern Africa, can still be found, though in limited numbers.

A hippopotamus, seen above emerging from the water in Mlilwane Wildlife Sanctuary, is drawn, like the crane, by the grain being spread. Mkhaya Wildlife Reserve features giraffes, seen below, that feed on acacia trees, common to savanna, or open grassland, in Africa. Ostriches (right) get to indulge their curiosity by inspecting visitors.

The Swazi people make up the largest Bantu group in the region. They have occupied the area now known as Swaziland for only the last two hundred years.

Chapter 2

THE EARLY PEOPLE

Artifacts found by anthropologists reveal that the Swaziland area was inhabited by people during the Early Stone Age, two million years ago. Tools have been found that show the presence of early humans in many of the valleys of Swaziland. Stone quarries tell the story of more recent habitation, 100,000 years ago.

More recently, hunter-gatherers have left evidence of their lives in the form of ostrich eggshell necklaces, bones shaped into needles, and other natural materials used to create rock paintings that tell of their life. They were followed by the San, also known as Bushmen, who lived throughout southern Africa. They made use of the natural environment but did not form any permanent settlements.

The arrival in the area of the first Bantu people from central Africa shaped the population of Swaziland as we know it today. Historians believe that these Nguni-speaking people began to move into the area about A.D. 400, bringing their farming skills with them. They may have been forced to migrate in the hunt for fresh grazing land for their animals. Or they may have been fleeing from more aggressive peoples. Whatever the reason for their arrival in Swaziland, they created permanent settlements and began to keep cattle.

The modern history of the Swazi people dates from the late fifteenth century when they migrated south, out of east-central

Africa, looking for better grazing land. Crossing the Limpopo River, they settled in what is today Mozambique, on the Indian Ocean, under their leader Dlamini. They remained there for more than two hundred years. These first Swazi people were known as the *bakaMswati* and *bakaNgwane*. The predominant language and culture of the people was Nguni.

INTO SWAZILAND

About the year 1750, King Ngwane III led his people inland across the Lubombo Mountains from Mozambique, to the land now called Swaziland. He was searching for a place that was secure, away from the African coast and the dangers posed by foreign sailors and explorers. They settled at the Pongola River,

Shaka, the Zulu warrior

in southern Swaziland, where he built his homestead, Lobamba. This is considered the birthplace and heart of the Swazi people.

Swazis who can trace their ancestors back to this king call themselves the people of Ngwane. Their nation is KaNgwane.

King Ngwane III was followed by his son, Ndvungunya, and his grandson, Sobhuza I. It was during the reign of Sobhuza I, who died in 1836, that the Swazis came up against Shaka, a Zulu warrior who set out to destroy neighboring peoples. His ferocity and his skill at both fighting and leading his people created an era known in southern Africa as *mfecane*, which means "time of crushing." Many peoples were crushed during his reign and many others were absorbed into the Zulu nation. King Sobhuza, rather than see his people absorbed, decided to lead them northward, away from the Zulus and also away from a rival chief, Zwide.

King Sobhuza I consolidated his power in the new region and strengthened the Dlamini clan. Although many of the people who followed him were not descendants of the Nguni, they became known as the true Swazi. Even today, only a Dlamini can become king of Swaziland. There are many royal princes and princesses named Dlamini, but not all Dlaminis are descended from royalty.

Sobhuza I built his home at Lobamba, in the center of Swaziland. But this was not far enough away to protect him from Shaka and Shaka's brother, Dingaan. Sobhuza tried to create an alliance with Shaka by sending two of his daughters to become Shaka's wives, but Dingaan stormed into Swaziland with his army in 1828. Sobhuza fled to the hills into secret caves where he was safe. There he lived until his death, when he was succeeded by his

Today, the Swazi king, Mswati III, shown at right, is on good terms with the Zulu King Goodwill Zwelithini, at left.

son, Mswati. By 1838, after Dingaan and his Zulu warriors were defeated by white settlers, the Swazis were able to stand up to a greatly weakened Zulu force.

KING MSWATI II

King Mswati II was just sixteen years old when he inherited the leadership of Swaziland in 1840, after his father's death. As is traditional in the Swazi royal family, the queen mother stood in for her son until he was mature enough to assume the throne.

King Mswati II was considered Swaziland's greatest fighting king. The very name "Swazi" is derived from his name. During the quarter century of his rule, he had to fight the Zulus as well as his own brothers. He conquered some groups and integrated them into Swazi society. These people came to be known as *Emafikamuva*—those who came late. King Mswati strengthened the loyalty of the people by adopting the practice of "age regiments." These "armies" of young men ignored the more usual ties of region and kinship and focused on creating fighting forces of men of the same age. They were the first Swazi forces known for their military skill and their discipline, two of the qualities that had made Shaka such a formidable enemy.

King Mswati II introduced Christianity to Swaziland by inviting missionaries to come and bring with them *umculu*, the "word." This idea began with his father, Sobhuza I, who had a dream about the "word" being brought by white men. This was interpreted to mean that missionaries would bring the Bible and its teaching to the Swazi people.

King Mswati united many different clans into a nation during

Roman Catholic missionaries, traveling in protected groups, made their mark in southern Africa during the nineteenth century. More than half of all Swazis are Christians.

his reign. Together, these people became known as *bakaMswati*, the people of Mswati. Eventually, the people became known as the Swazi and their country was called Swaziland. Swaziland is unusual in that few nations in Africa have just one culture in the entire population.

CREATING WEALTH

Mswati II built up his personal wealth in the form of cattle and by taking captives during warfare. During his reign, the practice of *lobola*, or bridewealth, was instituted. When a princess was to be given in marriage, the groom had to give the king a large number of cattle. This was far greater than the number required to marry any girl who was not of the royal family. The king could command any girl in the kingdom to become one of his wives, and her father had to provide a suitable number of cattle. It was not

The idea of cattle as wealth, instead of as food, was introduced by King Mswati II. Even today, cattle may be given to a bride's family on her marriage, increasing the rural family's wealth.

possible to refuse the king, and many girls became part of the royal household. The resulting concentration of cattle made the Dlamini clan the wealthiest in the region. It reinforced the idea that the king of the Swazis should have more wives, more cattle, and more land than anyone else.

The king staged a series of raids on neighboring lands, attacking the Sotho people who lived to the south, in the Transvaal area of South Africa. He gained more wealth as he took the property of those he conquered and added this land to the Swazi kingdom. His territory eventually reached as far north as the Limpopo River and to the Pongola River in the south. It reached the Indian Ocean to the east, and stretched far to the west, nearly to the boundary of the Orange Free State in South Africa. He also created new regiments for his army, ensuring his own safety.

But while the king was occupied fighting other black peoples, he found himself up against a very different group of people who were also interested in the land he had conquered.

One woman takes the lead in a dance being performed by the many royal wives of the king. They are wearing a traditional Swazi cloth.

A simple fence marks the border between South Africa and Swaziland. However, the differences between the two cultures are much greater than the fence indicates.

Chapter 3

WHITES ENTER SWAZILAND

The newcomers to the Swaziland region were the Boers, white farmers of Dutch descent. Although Mswati II conquered land, the land rarely had many people living on it, so he did not see the Boers as enemies. He thought they could provide a buffer between his own people and the black nations that surrounded them. A large block of territory was granted to the Dutch under their leader, Andries Potgieter. In acknowledgment of this grant, Potgieter agreed to give the Swazis one hundred head of cattle.

Land in what is now the eastern Transvaal—land that had historically been an invasion route of the Zulus—was ceded to the Boers in 1845. Ten years later, another large area was granted, this time in the northwest part of the Transvaal.

Misunderstandings then arose because of the African attitude toward land. Land could not be bought or sold because no single individual owned it. The land belonged to all the people and was there to be used. It was, and is, one of the responsibilities of the chiefs to allocate land to the people they ruled. As village populations grew, the pressure for more land increased. Sometimes the available land could not fill this need. One part of the community would then move on into a new area.

A typical Boer farm in southern Africa was recorded in this old engraving.

Therefore, in making the land grant, the Swazis meant only to give the Boers permission to settle. They did not mean actually to sell the land. However, the paper the Boers presented to Mswati, and which he signed, was an actual deed of sale.

When King Mswati died in 1865, a ten-year period of turmoil began. The land grants he had made to the Boers did not prevent Zulu raids. They came across the Pongola River, burned one of the royal homesteads, and seized cattle.

Further disruption came with the death of Mswati's son, Ludvonga, who had been named to succeed him. Orderly succession of kings was vital to the nation's well-being. In Swazi culture, any one of the king's sons may be selected to follow him, as long as the son is not married. The choice is often made according to the son's character and youth. If the chosen one is too young, he is named the crown prince and is given a period of time to learn his important new role. During that time, the queen mother and the former king's brother rule together. But the death of Ludvonga caused confusion. It delayed until 1875 the crowning of a new king, Mbandzeni, another of Mswati's sons.

Four hundred Boers attended the coronation to show they were the protectors of the Swazis. The Swazis needed such protection, for they were soon at the center of other people's battles.

WHITES FIGHT OVER LAND

The Boers and the British struggled for domination over the Transvaal, which nearly surrounded Swaziland. The Boers wanted to expand their territory to escape from British rule. The British were determined to spread their rule over the whole of

southern Africa. In 1877, the British forcibly annexed the Transvaal to their colony of South Africa.

The British had ongoing problems with the Zulus, who resisted British demands to give up their sovereignty. After the British were defeated by the Zulus in 1878 at the Battle of

A British soldier is seen by an artist as "Saving the Queen's Colors" during the devastating Battle of Isandhlwana against the Zulus.

Isandhlwana, they turned to the Swazis for help. King Mbandzeni sent eight thousand soldiers to help the British in their fight against the Pedi people, who were fighting to remain in the same territory. Although the Swazis suffered great losses, they won the battle. As a reward, the British guaranteed the Swazis' right to rule themselves. They even repealed the annexation of the Transvaal in 1881 and recognized Swaziland's independence, though they continued to claim the land for their livestock.

The discovery of valuable minerals in Swaziland—first gold and then tin—drew many people seeking the right, or concession, to search for these minerals. Again, a misunderstanding arose.

King Mbandzeni believed he was granting them only a limited right. The concessionaires believed they were acquiring the permanent right to the land and anything they found on it. The number of concession-seekers grew so large that the king needed a trusted white advisor who understood the white men but would keep the best interests of the Swazi people in mind.

The king turned to Sir Theophilus Shepstone, a trusted white man who had served other African kings well. The king asked Shepstone to send him one of his sons to look after Swazi interests. This son, also named Theophilus Shepstone, arrived early in 1887 to take up his duties.

The younger Shepstone found a web of conflicting and over-lapping concessions. Licenses had been granted for virtually every form of business including manufacturing, collecting customs duties, printing, and even pawnbroking. The king and his council had signed away virtually the entire country, including the possibility of profiting from development in the future.

The Swazis summed it all up by saying, "The documents killed

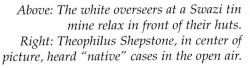

Above: The white overseers at a Swazi tin mine relax in front of their huts.
Right: Theophilus Shepstone, in center of picture, heard "native" cases in the open air.

us." It is unclear why the king allowed all the concessions, but Shepstone failed to improve the situation, either through incompetence or for his own profit. The Swazi monarchy acquired wealth from the concessions, but the people become completely dependent on the labor of others.

The five hundred whites living in Swaziland felt they should be able to deal with their own affairs. They did not want to be subject to the king or to Shepstone as his agent. In 1888 King Mbandzeni granted this group a charter allowing for their self-government. He still held a veto over any decisions that did not meet with his approval. It was a strange compromise, allowing for two governments within the same territory. It didn't work.

CONFLICT BETWEEN WHITES

The Boers and the British continued to argue over Swaziland, each claiming its side was protecting the king. Ultimately, the

He wont be happy 'till he gets it!

Paul Kruger (left), president of the Transvaal, was known to be determined to "protect" Swaziland into his Boer-run domain, as shown by a political cartoon printed at the time.

British and the Transvaal governments created a commission to decide the future of Swaziland even though the Swazi king protested that they had no right to make such a decision.

Shepstone was removed from his position for a brief time and was replaced by Allister Miller, a British journalist. Although Miller did not hold an official position for long, he remained an advisor to the king and lived in Swaziland for the rest of his life. He is said to have been responsible for the Swazi monarchy losing a lot of land.

King Mbandzeni became ill and died in late 1889, at the age of thirty-four. During the year following his death, President Paul Kruger of the Transvaal and Sir Henry Loch, the British High Commissioner, met with Cecil Rhodes, an ambitious British businessman who had his own vision for the region. Under Rhodes's influence, Loch allowed the Transvaal to take over a portion of the Swazis' land. Then the Swaziland Convention of 1894 turned the country into a political dependency of the

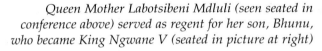

Queen Mother Labotsibeni Mdluli (seen seated in conference above) served as regent for her son, Bhunu, who became King Ngwane V (seated in picture at right)

Transvaal, as a result of Rhodes's desire to have a clear path from Cape Town in South Africa right into central Africa.

All this maneuvering was taking place during the time that Swaziland was under the stewardship of Queen Mother Labotsibeni Mdluli. She was the acting head of state in place of her son, Bhunu. Bhunu became King Ngwane V in 1894 at the age of eighteen. His brief reign came during years when Swaziland's very survival as an independent state was constantly in question.

THE PROTECTORATE THAT DIDN'T PROTECT

In 1894 two dramatic events changed the course of Swazi history. Against the strong opposition of the Swazis, the British allowed Swaziland to be named a protectorate of the Transvaal, effectively placing it under the control of their old enemies, the Boers.

Swazi workers joined South Africans working at this South African gold mine, seen here in 1888, only two years after gold was discovered.

At the same time, the Swazis' cattle herds were struck by the deadly disease known as rinderpest. It killed virtually all of their livestock. Without their animals, the Swazis were without economic resources. This period became known as the "eating up of the land" because so much territory was lost. By 1897 Sir Alfred Milner, British High Commissioner for South Africa, viewed the entire southern Africa region as far north as the Zambezi River as a European "preserve." In his view, the only role the African people had to play was as a labor force in the vast gold fields that had been discovered in South Africa in 1886.

One way to force the Africans into working in the mines was by imposing taxes on them that had to be paid in cash. In 1897 a tax was set by the Transvaal government that had to be paid by every adult man and woman. Mine work was the only work available that paid wages. The Swazis found themselves forced to work to pay taxes merely to be allowed to live in their own homes, on what had once been their own land. This "head tax" policy was adopted by colonial powers throughout Africa in order to force Africans into wage-earning work.

This was the start of a pattern that saw Swazi men leaving home for long periods of time to work in the mines. It disrupted family life as well as Swazi cultural life. The chain of authority and the relations within families were severely affected. Swaziland became totally dependent on South Africa for its entire economic life.

King Bhunu's brief reign came to an end in 1899 when he collapsed during a ceremony and died. Because he was just in his twenties, all of his children were very young. The royal council that decides such matters chose one of his sons, a four-month-old infant, as heir to the throne. As was the custom, Queen Regent Labotsibeni—the boy's grandmother—ruled in his place, assisted by her son, Malunge. She ruled from 1899 to 1921, when the new king was old enough to assume the throne.

ANGLO-BOER WAR

There is a saying in Africa that when the elephants fight, the grass suffers. The same could be said of a small country that happens to be in the path of two warring factions. The hostility between the Boers and the English-speaking whites of South Africa turned into warfare on October 11, 1899, and continued on

A British artist preserved the action in the Anglo-Boer War in 1900.

and off until the Boers surrendered in March 1901. British forces marched through Swaziland and fought on Swazi soil. At one point, an officer fighting on the British side made his base at Lomahasha and raided the township of Bremersdorp (now called Manzini). Other settlements were also raided as the British sought supplies and searched for Europeans living in Swaziland. They even took Prince Mancibane, a Swazi chief, as a prisoner because it was believed he was helping the Boers.

Through all of this, the Swazis tried to remain neutral, calling it "a white man's war." Their determination was severely tested when most of Bremersdorp, the administrative capital of Swaziland, was burned to the ground by the Boers. At the same time, they found Prince Mancibane and released him.

The headquarters of the British in Bremersdorp (later called Manzini) was burned by the Boers from South Africa.

BRITAIN TAKES OVER

When the war came to an end with the defeat of the Boers and the signing of a peace treaty on May 31, 1902, the British took control of the Transvaal. The British government also assumed control over Swaziland under the pretense of being its protector. However, Swaziland never received official status as either a protectorate, a colony, or a possession. But the lack of a title did not deter the British from imposing extremely harsh conditions on the people. They set about stripping the Swazi people of their land, their freedom, and their identity as a nation.

This task was carried out by individuals such as Alfred Milner, then governor of the Transvaal. In 1906 he declared, "It is my opinion that the Swazi must be freed from the exclusiveness of tribal life." This was a way of saying that Swazi traditions were going to come to an end. The first step toward making this happen was taken in 1907 when Swaziland was partitioned into "native" and European areas. The Swazis were allowed just one-third of the territory. Another third was awarded to whites for their own use, and the last third was held in reserve as Crown Land.

Even the land allotted to the Swazis was not entirely their own. Although it was believed that most of the minerals would be found in areas allocated to whites, any minerals that might exist on Swazi land also belonged to the colonial power. Europeans had the right to prospect for such minerals and to develop them. Any Swazis living on what then became European land were expected to stay there and become laborers for the whites.

Swazi land was the poorest in the country. About 15 percent of it was suitable for farming, while nearly three-quarters of the land granted to white settlers was good farmland. The Swazis, bitter over the division of their land, made every effort to fight it.

In preparation for the partition, control of Swaziland was transferred from the governor of the Transvaal to Lord Selborne, the new British High Commissioner for South Africa. The Swazis petitioned Lord Selborne to change the conditions of the partition. Instead of agreeing to any changes, Selborne appointed a resident commissioner to be stationed in Swaziland at Mbabane, the capital.

The Partition Proclamation went into effect in 1907, and the Swazis were left with just 40 percent of their land. They did not receive any compensation for the land taken from them. During the next several decades, their official protests were ignored.

SOUTH AFRICA TIGHTENS CONTROL

Swaziland was now being viewed by the British as a natural part of the Union of South Africa. They worked to denationalize the Swazi people, that is, to take away their identity and way of living and to make the territory into a self-governing white community. The Swazis were seen merely as an available labor force. Lord Milner believed that Swaziland could not be separated economically from South Africa. Under that reasoning, it was clearly only a matter of time before Swaziland would be made part of the Union of South Africa. Although this did not actually happen, the economic ties were a reality. Young men by the tens of thousands went to work in South Africa's gold mines.

As the queen regent, Labotsibeni fought against the loss of Swazi land and the forced removal of Swazis to reserves that were created by the British. She had a practical plan to get back Swazi land. She urged young Swazi men to work in the gold mines but asked that they contribute a portion of their earnings to a fund to buy back the land that was taken from them. This request became a demand. Although taxes had first been imposed by the Europeans, it was the Swazi queen who heavily burdened the Swazi people with taxes. So many men went to the mines that Swaziland became a nation of migrant laborers. Coupled with the loss of farmland, this migration caused such a complete disruption of normal family life that the country lost its ability to feed itself. It became a regular importer of such basic foods as grain. This need simply increased its dependence on South Africa.

By 1920, it was estimated that 25 to 40 percent of all Swazi men between the ages of eighteen and forty-five were working in the mines of the Transvaal or on South African farms. Many Swazi men also found work within Swaziland, on white-owned ranches and commercial farms. This also contributed to the deterioration of the Swazis' own food production.

For decades, border posts saw a heavy flow of Swazis going to work in South Africa and South Africans escaping the harshness of apartheid at home.

To the British colonial office, it was only a matter of time before Swaziland was made part of South Africa. In 1927 Colonial Secretary L.S. Amery said, "The key to the policy of timely transfer was to make Swaziland effectively British before it goes into the Union." It was considered a mistake to make this move before a prosperous and content British community had been established.

British institutions formed the basis for this community. Bus lines connecting the main settlements with South Africa, roads, irrigation projects, and communications were all directed toward the settlers. Education for whites, which had started in Bremersdorp in 1894, was expanded. As in South Africa, the British established a completely segregated school system, with separate facilities for blacks, people of mixed race, and whites.

The queen regent was determined to see that the crown prince was educated the way the white men were. She felt that the power of the whites came from "their money and books. We too will learn," she said. "We too will be rich." She established a special school at Zombodze near her royal residence for the education of the crown prince, who was known as Sobhuza II.

After his primary education was completed, he was sent to Lovedale College in the Cape Province of South Africa. In order to finance both the school and the young king's further education, every Swazi taxpayer was required to contribute a specific sum of money every year.

When Sobhuza II went to school, he was accompanied by a number of his comrades, representing all levels of Swazi life. For those boys whose parents could not afford to send them, the national education fund paid their way. This kept Sobhuza in touch with his people, despite his superior education.

King Sobhuza II, seen here at about eighteen years of age, lived to become the longest reigning monarch on earth.

Sobhuza II, king of Swaziland, seen here in his memorial at Lobamba, took his people from being subjects of the British crown in 1921 to independence in 1968. He then lived another fourteen years, helping the Swazi people to regain some of their land.

Chapter 4

SOBHUZA II AND INDEPENDENCE

On December 22, 1921, Sobhuza II was installed as king of the Swazi people, although the British insisted that he be called the "paramount chief." He was truly the king, however, and went on to rule through much of the twentieth century. Unlike his predecessors, Sobhuza II lived a very long life and ruled from 1921 until his death in 1982 at the age of eighty-three. His rule was not only of long duration but was also a remarkable blend of tradition and adaptation to modern life.

SWAZILAND FOR THE SWAZIS

Sobhuza II was determined to reclaim the land that had been taken away from his people. He used the land issue as a bargaining device, suggesting a willingness to join the Union of South Africa in exchange for land. The growing Swazi population was getting desperate for land for farming and pasture. By the start of World War II, conditions in the Native Areas were very harsh. Because Great Britain needed the support of its colonies in its war against Germany, it began to change its treatment of Swaziland.

In 1940, funds were granted for Swazis to repurchase land held

Signs throughout South Africa made clear that the nation's policy was one of apartheid, or separation of the races, until the 1990s.

by the Europeans. In addition, the Colonial Office gave back to the Swazis some of the Crown Land. At the same time, the king imposed a tax on Swazi cattle in order to buy back even more land.

By 1946 the Native Land Settlement Scheme saw a total of 350,000 acres (141,642 hectares) of land returned to the Swazis.

In spite of South Africa's many attempts to incorporate Swaziland into the Union of South Africa, Sobhuza II held firm. With the establishment of the apartheid government in South Africa in 1948, which decreed a strict separation of the races, Britain transferred control of Swaziland and its other territories to the Colonial Office.

During the previous three decades, Swaziland had stagnated. It was truly a forgotten colony. No roads had been built, no railroads introduced, no airports established. Cattle were subject to frequent attacks of hoof-and-mouth disease, and few doctors were available to treat the human population. More than 40 percent of the land remained in white hands though whites made up only 3 percent of the population.

In 1953 Sobhuza II attended the coronation of Queen Elizabeth II in London. He became a popular figure with the press.

ADMINISTERING THE COLONY

Although Swaziland was ruled by the king, most of the major decisions about the welfare of the people were made under the Native Administration Proclamations of 1944 and 1950. The first such act was so contrary to traditional Swazi law and customs that the Colonial Office was obliged to change it so as to take away some of the powers that had been designated for the resident commissioner. The Swazis insisted that only the *ngwenyama*—the king—had the authority to rule on matters affecting their administration. The second proclamation gave the ngwenyama these powers but only with the approval of the resident commissioner.

King Sobhuza II traveled to London in 1953 to attend the coronation of Queen Elizabeth II. This journey was a great undertaking, and the king was accompanied by many members of the royal family. Although Swaziland was still just a colony of Great Britain, and a very small one at that, the Swazi king enjoyed as much status among his people as the Queen of England did among hers. Since the British royal family had visited Swaziland just six years earlier during their fourteen-week journey to South Africa, the princess who had just been crowned Queen of England had vivid memories of that trip.

THE PUSH FOR INDEPENDENCE

In Swaziland, the desire for political independence was intense. This desire was reinforced by the fact that South Africa's prime minister, Dr. Hendrik Verwoerd, was still trying to make the protectorate part of his country and to destroy the Swazis' identity as a people and a nation.

But Verwoerd was hanging onto the past while the rest of Africa was moving toward the future. Britain's other two protectorates, Botswana and Lesotho, were both moving ahead of Swaziland. They gained their independence in 1966.

Britain began the process of establishing a commission to look into the question of Swazi independence, but King Sobhuza II jumped ahead and made his own presentation. Meetings were

On a cold day in January 1963, Swazi delegates to a constitutional conference in London arrived wearing their native dress.

Sixty-nine-year-old King Sobhuza II reviewed members of the First Battalion Malawi Rifles during independence celebrations in 1968.

held throughout 1960 and 1961 to discuss ways of bringing self-rule to Swaziland. The country would need a constitution, the rights of whites and blacks had to be agreed on, and the question of who would represent the Swazi people in the final discussions with Great Britain had to be decided. Another two years of debate passed before a constitution was ready. Even this document contained many clauses that were not in agreement with Swazi law and customs.

The process set up for voting on the constitution was heavily weighted on the side of the Europeans. Although they made up only a tiny part of the population, they were given one-third of the votes on the legislative council. The rules regarding eligibility for voting were also made according to European custom. For example, although some Swazi men had more than one wife, only one wife from each household was allowed to vote.

Another three years passed while the legislative council did its work. Finally, a general election to create the nation's first parliament was held in April 1967. On April 24, 1967, Sobhuza II

Swazi laborers worked on a major hydroelectric project, financed by the World Bank, in the 1960s.

was officially installed as King of Swaziland, and Swaziland was officially made a protectorate of the United Kingdom. These steps were necessary in order to move toward the actual moment of independence.

Last-minute discussions about mineral rights threatened to delay independence, but it finally came on September 6, 1968. Swaziland immediately became a member of both the United Nations and the Organization of African Unity, signaling its entry into the world of independent nations.

CREATING A MODERN NATION

King Sobhuza II now faced the enormous job of merging the old Swaziland with the idea of its new political form as an independent nation. One of the biggest tasks was to resolve the issue of the land that had been sold off by the British during their administration of the territory. There was little dispute about the illegal manner in which the land had been sold by the British. However, the British had claimed vast areas of Africa in the name of the queen, and in most cases, the original inhabitants of those regions never got their land back. In Swaziland, however, the Swazi National Council convinced the British to return land to the Swazi people. Although this did not happen overnight, by 1980 a British Fund created for this purpose had bought more than 200,000 acres (80,938 hectares) of land to be turned back to the Swazi people.

During this same period, a committee was established to look after the country's mineral rights, which had also been taken away during the British period. This committee was known as *Tibiyo takaNgwane,* words that mean "minerals of Swaziland" in siSwati, the Swazi language. Its mission was broader than just reclaiming mineral rights. It was given a charter by King Sobhuza to improve the standard of living and education of the Swazi people.

Within ten years, Tibiyo takaNgwane had bought back 100,000 acres (40,469 hectares) of land and turned part of this land over for various national projects. Scholarships were established for high school students and for study abroad. The committee invested in the country's economy, including mining, sugarcane, meat, freight, and agriculture.

A NEW GOVERNMENT

Swaziland had inherited a political system based largely on Great Britain's, which had very little to do with the Swazi culture or experience. The idea of having different political parties

As Swazi independence approached, the world's press found the king's many wives a subject of great interest. One paper wondered whether this wife, shown with her daughter, might be eligible to be called the "First Lady."

working toward a common goal was completely outside the Swazi tradition. In 1972, when it was time for general elections, the first since independence, there was a growing desire to find a system that was more in keeping with the Swazi way of doing things. During these elections, members of the king's own political party, the Imbokodvo Party, lost a number of seats in the government, including that of cabinet minister.

The king, who had by then ruled his people for 52 years, the longest reign in the world, found this intolerable. To govern as he saw fit, he needed to have complete control. On April 12, 1973, he repealed Swaziland's constitution, which he said was founded on a British model not appropriate for Swaziland. He also dissolved the parliament and barred all political parties. He feared that the trade unions would pose a threat to his power unless he outlawed any organized protests.

There is disagreement about these dramatic and autocratic actions, but the king has been seen by most people as acting in what he believed were the best interests of the people. Undeniably he set democracy back many steps and demonstrated his intention to maintain tight control over the country he ruled for so long.

Immediately, however, the king established a Royal

Constitutional Commission that was instructed to go to all the corners of the kingdom to find out what the people wanted their constitution to be. The commission also visited other countries in Africa and in Europe to study their constitutions. It concluded that Swaziland should have a parliament with two houses but no political parties at all. After these findings, several years passed during which King Sobhuza did not act on the recommendations.

Instead, he revived the tradition of councils known as *tinkhundla*. The councils were run with the cooperation of the local chiefs. Sobhuza made the tinkhundla system more organized and gave it more importance. In 1978, a statement was finally issued regarding the establishment of a new parliament. The election of members to parliament had to go through the slow tinkhundla system. By turning the clock back to an earlier time, Sobhuza was able to concentrate power in his own hands.

In place of the constitution he had thrown out five years before, Sobhuza proclaimed a new constitution on October 13, 1978. However, the actual document was never published and the people never knew what it said. Even after forty people were elected to the first parliament, the king had the right to add ten of his own candidates who did not have to be elected.

In spite of this tight control, the king had made it clear that anyone in Swaziland was eligible for office, and of the fifty new members of Parliament, six were white and four were women.

King Sobhuza II continued to rule the country until his death in August 1982 at the age of eighty-three. He had governed for sixty years, bringing Swaziland out of the colonial period through independence and into the modern era. With his death, the stage was set for the unique Swazi tradition of identifying the next king.

King Mswati III, successor to Sobhuza II, making a formal, traditional appearance, stands before his people at the National Stadium, bearing the Swazi

Chapter 5

A ROYAL LIFE

King Sobhuza II had been on the throne for so long that there were few people with clear memories of the rituals to be followed in choosing a king and seeing him through the coronation. When Sobhuza was already in his eighties, he recognized that much had changed since he had become king. He made an effort to change the running of the *liqoqo,* or royal council, which had ruled informally. This body, made up of about twenty to thirty members, including princes of the royal family as well as a few chiefs from among the commoners, would discuss matters of importance until a consensus was reached. Then the king would announce their decision as if it were his sole command.

The king of Swaziland acts in three different areas of government, known in the western world as the legislative, executive, and judicial branches. Sobhuza felt there was a need for the liqoqo to be modernized and made into a more formal body so that there would be more continuity after his death. But he died before he could act. As a result, there was confusion about which ministers were officially in charge of the kingdom.

CHOOSING A KING

In many monarchies, such as Great Britain, the heir to the throne is always the monarch's first-born son, or first-born daughter if there is no son. In the Netherlands, the heir is the first-born child of either sex. However, in Swaziland the heir is chosen from among all the king's sons. The boy's position as heir is not known when he is born, so there is no long period while he waits to become king. He goes about his normal life until the moment he is chosen.

There are many possible candidates for the throne because the king has many wives and thus many children. While very few other men in Swaziland have more than one wife, it has been the rule that the king takes many, many wives. This is a tradition that seems out of step with modern life, yet it is still being followed. No one is supposed to know how many wives and children the king has, but King Sobhuza was believed to have had more than seventy wives and well over one hundred sons.

The royal council has the task of choosing a son who has already exhibited the qualities that would make him a good ruler while he is still young enough to be properly educated and trained for the position. The process actually begins by choosing a queen mother from among the late king's wives. Because she will rule along with her son, her abilities and character are at least as important as his. Her standing within the family is the most important quality. If she should die while her son is king, which is likely and which was the case during the reign of Sobhuza II, she must be replaced immediately by one of her sisters.

The new king must be unmarried when crowned because a king's wives are not chosen in the ordinary manner. It is also a Swazi tradition that a king may not be succeeded by his own brothers. To be sure this cannot happen, the mother of the chosen king is not allowed to have another son. So, despite the official

Makhosetive, who became King Mswati III, was chosen when he was fourteen to succeed Sobhuza II.

secrecy surrounding the choice of king, it is clear that a child has been singled out by the royal family's inner circle when he is just a baby.

At the time of King Sobhuza's death, the queen mother was Dzeliwe, his eldest wife, and it was she who took over the reins of the kingdom. She was officially installed in office as queen regent of Swaziland at a ceremony held before King Sobhuza's funeral. There were strong traditions that Queen Mother Dzeliwe was expected to follow, but she had her own ideas, especially in wanting the crown prince to be educated abroad. She was opposed in this by Prince Sozisa who was to act in her behalf should she be unable to carry out the duties of her office. Prince Sozisa believed that the crown prince was too young to be sent abroad, particularly since he had not completed certain traditional rituals.

THE NEW KING

In 1982, the royal inner council made its choice known: Sobhuza II would be succeeded by fourteen-year-old Makhosetive, the son of Queen Ntombi. As soon as he was selected, he was taken to a secluded place, and a royal homestead was created for him not far from Lobamba, the royal residence.

Queen Dzeliwe succeeded in sending the crown prince to England. He was accompanied by other members of the royal family and by Swaziland's minister of education. After the crown prince's departure, Dzeliwe addressed the chiefs of the kingdom but did not reveal that the prince had been sent away to England. This secrecy caused much dissension and bitterness in the kingdom.

Queen Mother Dzeliwe dismissed the entire liqoqo, or royal inner council, including Prince Sozisa. This action went against the very core of Swazi tradition because the king rules in cooperation with the liqoqo. In addition, all Swazi traditional life revolves around the king and his mother. As a result, senior members of the royal house of Dlamini took an unprecedented step. They removed Queen Dzeliwe from office and informed the nation, through the national radio station, of the identity of the crown prince. It was the first time that he was officially identified as the heir to the throne. The people were also told that the crown prince was away in England.

QUEEN REGENT NTOMBI

Although the crown prince's mother, Queen Ntombi, was still observing the official period of mourning, it was important that she be installed in office, in place of Queen Dzeliwe. In Swazi custom, the crown prince may not come into contact with anyone still observing mourning. In order to avoid this, the outward signs of the queen's mourning were removed.

Queen Regent Ntombi, mother of Crown Prince Makhosetive, ruled and oversaw his education until he was old enough to become king.

With Queen Regent Ntombi now installed, Crown Prince Makhosetive was brought back to the kingdom. At a ceremony held at the Somhlolo National Stadium, he was formally presented to the Swazi people on September 12, 1983. He was fifteen years old, exactly the same age as the country he was to rule, and many people believe that he was chosen in part because he was born in the year of independence.

Although the crown prince wore Western clothes in England, for this important occasion he wore the traditional Swazi cloth known as *emahiya*. In his hair he placed the red feathers of the lourie bird. Only members of the royal family may wear these red feathers. Shortly after the ceremony, the crown prince returned to England to study for one more year.

Without the strong hand of King Sobhuza steering the nation, political dissension grew, and conflicting declarations were made by various members of the ruling bodies.   The stability of King Sobhuza's long reign had, in many ways, left his people unprepared for change.

As political maneuvering continued, it was clear that action had to be taken. The mourning period for King Sobhuza was declared at an end after only two years, rather than the traditional three. The main house in the women's section of the royal homestead at Lobamba was removed to a new location a short distance away. This was the beginning of the creation of a new royal homestead for the new king. The homestead was built by men and women who came from all over the kingdom to perform this task. Building the homestead is one of the most important roles they play. It was here that the new king would undergo all the ceremonies appropriate to his position. Also at this time, the crown prince took the name Mswati III.

THE LIFE OF A KING

Traditionally, the Swazi king is known as both the father of the nation and the child of the people. When he ascends to the throne, he is known as *ingwenyama,* which means "lion." The queen mother is given cattle, for she is now the mother of the country. She is known as *indlovukati,* the "lady elephant."

At fifteen, Makhosetive came back to Swaziland to complete

King Mswati III (left) in his military uniform, appearing at the Royal Residence at Ebuhleni, sits next to his mother, Queen Mother Ntombi.

his formal education and to undergo the rites that would turn him into a king. He came under the guidance of the headmaster of Waterford Kamhlaba School, who set up a special program of tutoring for him, one that would instill a moral code in the young man who would soon be responsible for the well-being of all the Swazi people. At the same time, he was also going through

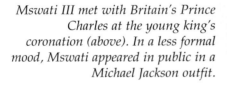

Mswati III met with Britain's Prince Charles at the young king's coronation (above). In a less formal mood, Mswati appeared in public in a Michael Jackson outfit.

traditional Swazi rituals including the important *sibhimbi sekutfomba*, a celebration of his achieving maturity.

The crowning of Makhosetive as King Mswati III was done in great secrecy. Only his close advisors were present for the secret rites. The king's royal position is marked by wearing red lourie feathers in his hair and leopard skins during important public appearances. He may also wear traditional Swazi cloth.

The day after the secret ceremonies, the king emerged to be greeted by the regiments that had come to pay tribute to him. He made his first public appearance as king, carrying a shield made of cowhide and a traditional stick. The gathering took place in the newly built enclosure within the national cattle *kraal* (enclosure) made of tree limbs at the new royal village in the Ezulwini Valley, the traditional home of the Swazi royal family.

The following day, a public celebration was held at Somhlolo National Stadium. High-ranking representatives of governments

The royal wives appear in public at the Somhlolo National Stadium, dancing during a ceremony.

from other African countries as well as from Europe and the United States were among the 100,000 joyous people attending this celebration. A performance of traditional dancing and singing was held before the king made his first speech.

THE KING'S WIVES

The rituals surrounding the king's wives are very disturbing to many modern people in Swaziland, and are out of step with every aspect of contemporary life, both in Swaziland and the rest of the region. There are official wives, each of whom has a specific function. The king's first wife, known as his ritual wife, is doomed to a life of loneliness because she is not permitted to have any children. She is considered to belong to the entire royal family and is seen as an extension of the new king.

King Mswati III seems destined to amass even more wives than his late father did. By the time he was twenty-five years old, he already had at least five wives, although officially, no one knows the actual number. For the families of these girls, marriage to the king is a very mixed blessing. Essentially, they lose their daughters. The royal wives have little contact with other people. Their children also are kept apart, and may have no contact with their mother's family at all.

But beyond the question of the number of wives, this king is known to desire many women. He has often taken an interest in a girl who has no interest in joining the royal household. But since it is impossible to say no to the king, even in modern times, the only recourse for some of these girls has been to leave the country for a period of time.

THE REED DANCE

When King Sobhuza ruled the country, he would choose a new wife every year at the annual Reed Dance. This is one of the two most important ceremonies of the Swazi people. He continued this practice until he was in his seventies. Some girls avoided the chance of being chosen by staying away from the dance on the day he would make his choice known.

The Reed Dance, or *umhlanga,* is held in September each year. This dance is really a week-long series of events, all of them focusing on the unmarried girls of the kingdom, known as maidens. From all over the nation, girls come to the region where tall reeds may be gathered to rebuild the fence around the queen mother's residence. The timing of the Reed Dance is tied to the maturing of the reeds.

Thousands of girls take part each year, with the youngest ones going to reed-gathering sites closest to the kraal. After cutting the

The maidens who participate in the annual Reed Dance gather tall reeds and then rebuild the queen mother's residence. The work is interspersed by several ceremonial dances. The king may choose a new wife during the week-long celebration.

reeds, the girls carry the bundles back to the vicinity of the Royal Kraal where they spend a day bathing in the natural warm springs. They prepare their hair and make last-minute adjustments to their costumes.

Each girl wears a tiny skirt decorated with colored beads. She is bare-breasted, as is traditional among unmarried Swazi girls. When a woman marries, she covers her breasts, which are then associated with child-bearing.

Across the girl's chest she wears a scarf of brightly colored wool, knotted into balls or fringe. The colors—red, yellow, blue, and green—have specific meanings, tied to the relationship of the girl with her boyfriend. The primary requirement for any girl who wants to take part in the Reed Dance is that she must not have had a baby, so the message of the colors must be carefully considered.

Royal children are seldom seen by the public, but this one is getting an early experience in dressing in the colorful wool tassels worn for the Reed Dance.

While the king ritually chooses a bride at the Reed Dance, other members of royalty may also find brides during the week. The best-known outsider to find a bride at the Reed Dance is King Zwelithini, king of the Zulus of South Africa, who chose a Swazi princess to be his bride when he attended the Reed Dance in 1973.

No one may enter the Royal Kraal where the girls bring the reeds, so the first time the maidens are seen is when they come streaming out through the entrance. They form a seemingly endless sea of brown skin and brightly colored decorations, all in motion as they dance their way onto a field by the Royal Kraal.

The girls chant and follow the lead girl, who blows a whistle to keep them in order. Though the ceremony brings out thousands of participants, they dance as part of a whole, not as individual performers. To achieve this harmony, the girls practice together for a full day before they make their appearance. Girls come back to take part in the Reed Dance year after year until they marry.

THE NCWALA

The most significant ceremony, and the one most closely tied to the king, is the Ncwala, the ceremony of the first fruits. Not only

Young men of an age regiment wear traditional furs and skins during the Ncwala ritual, or ceremony of the first fruits.

does this ceremony mark the beginning of the harvest season, a moment of crucial importance in the life of every agricultural people, but it is also celebrated as a renewal of the king, who embodies the fruitfulness of the nation. For that reason, the ceremony is held only after a new king is installed and then during the life of that king. It is not held during the mourning period. It is also not held before a crown prince has come of age because it is considered inappropriate for a minor to celebrate an occasion devoted to fruitfulness.

The ceremony combines a celebration of the new year and a thanksgiving for the year that has just ended. It takes place over a month-long period, and is timed according to the phases of the

moon. The ceremony begins around October or November, when
the new moon is seen. This is springtime in the southern
hemisphere. Although the Ncwala has sacred qualities, it is also a
time of great joy.

Gathering water from two specific sources is an important part
of the ceremony. One group of "water priests" travels eastward to
the Indian Ocean, the ultimate outlet for all rivers that cross
Swaziland. A second group heads north toward three rivers whose
waters have come from the eastern Transvaal. That region is
particularly important because it was once Swazi territory. The
king himself sees to the departure of the water priests. These
young men must walk all the way. They are forbidden to accept
rides from passing vehicles. The round trip to gather the water
takes about two weeks.

This phase marks the beginning of the king's withdrawal from
public life. He remains secluded until the Ncwala is over. The
water gathering is followed by rituals involving particular herbs,
shrubs, and leaves. Boys whose older brothers are taking part in
the ceremony may start attending when they are only ten.

On the final day of the ceremony, a black ox must be caught by
the young men and killed. Traditionally brewed beer is served.
The king, emerging from seclusion, inspects the regiments and
joins in dancing. The end of this symbolic day is marked when a
gourd is thrown onto a shield near the king's sanctuary.

To conclude the ceremony, everything that has been used
during the week—the king's sanctuary, sleeping mats, clothing
and other objects—is burned in a huge fire. The old year is cast
away. The fire renews the land, making it ready for the new
growing cycle.

The Houses of Parliament are located in Lobamba, the royal village.

ROYAL VILLAGE OF LOBAMBA

Lobamba, the royal area of Swaziland, is situated between Mbabane and Manzini, on the main road. This is where King Mswati III maintains his official kraal and where the important ceremonies take place. The Somhlolo National Stadium, where public celebrations are held, is also located here. Significant anniversaries of the country's independence are celebrated here, such as the Tenth Anniversary when King Sobhuza presided over a great show of military men, marching in brilliant red uniforms. Visiting dignitaries are greeted in the stadium.

The Houses of Parliament are also in the complex and may be seen clearly from the main road. Parliament is open to visitors on guided tours. There includes the Upper House and House of Assembly. Debates take place in Swaziland's two official languages, English and siSwati. Because Swaziland was part of the British colonial system, English is widely spoken, especially in business.

The National Museum is located next to the Houses of Parliament. At the museum, visitors may see displays that explain Swazi dress and traditions as well as a series of photographs showing the nation's history.

Above: Fabrics, pottery, masks, and small sculptures are among the traditional craft objects made and sold by women.
Below: One of the traditional forms of housing is the beehive hut, made of woven reeds.

Chapter 6

DAILY LIFE

Although Swaziland has modern industries and small cities, more than half its people continue to live as subsistence farmers, growing only enough food for their own needs on small garden plots. They live under the close guidance of traditional chiefs who direct life on the local level. The basic family unit is an extended family group living under a headman. The family's living quarters are built to surround the cattle pen where the animals are kept at night. Every homestead is controlled jointly by the headman and his mother. She occupies her own house in the same compound; the son's grown children also have their own house where they stay until they are married.

Every aspect of the kraal is built according to tradition. The cattle kraal is built to face the rising sun; women are not allowed to enter it. A granary pit is dug to store the food, which is distributed by the headman. The great house, a meeting place, is under the control of the mother of the headman; she is also known as the chief woman. None of the other wives are allowed to enter this house, which is decorated with the skulls of cattle that have been sacrificed during rituals.

Separate rooms for sleeping or cooking and storing food are placed at specific points around the kraal. After living for a year under the chief woman, a newly married woman gets her own rooms and a yard. These rooms are built from local materials, so

Standing in front of the woven fence surrounding their kraal is a typical Swazi family.

they differ from one region to another. Dried grasses are used in the middle and high ranges, while in the wooded countryside, houses are made of branches and saplings.

When a man marries, he builds his home near his mother, who is then put in charge of his wife. If he has more than one wife, the kraal grows into a little village. Only a small percentage of Swazi men can afford to have more than one wife. The cost of lobola is too high a burden. Even fifty years ago, the respected researcher Hilda Kuper reported that fewer than one-fifth of Swazi men had more than one wife.

In village life, the chief is the law. No ordinary person may simply approach a chief; he must show respect. The land on which the chief lives, along with the families he rules, is land that was granted to his ancestors. These chiefdoms, also known as principalities, were given to the sons of kings dating back to the

This chief from a village in the Piggs Peak area is wearing ceremonial garb.

reign of Mswati I. Many of the chiefs are members of the royal family. These positions were passed down from father to son.

The chief knows each family on his land. Every important event is reported to him: every birth, every wedding, every death. He must be consulted about every aspect of daily life; he even decides when the people may plant their crops.

AGE SETS

Traditionally, young men are formed into age sets called regiments. From the age of about fifteen, men are formed into a new age set, and they form a unit whose loyalty is to their king and the nation. The idea of age sets is a familiar one in many areas of Africa. In Swaziland, it was introduced by King Mswati I. The regiment is unarmed, making it more like a national peace corps than an army. Going through the rituals bonds the men in lifelong friendship. When necessary, the men in an age set come to each other's aid. As the members of a regiment grow older and marry, a new regiment begins to form from the next group of young men. There is no comparable system for women.

The puberty rituals for men that were practiced in Swaziland for many generations had virtually disappeared during the colonial period when traditional life was strongly discouraged. When Sobhuza II reached puberty, a ceremony was re-created for him. A blood bond was established with a boy of his own age. They were considered to be bonded for life.

TRADITIONAL BELIEFS

Religion plays a large role in traditional Swazi life, though there is no specific religious figure such as a priest or a religious order. Swazis believe strongly in a spirit world that is closely tied to the day-to-day world. This belief carries throughout Swaziland, including the professional and educated class. According to the Swazis, approximately 80 percent of the people consult traditional healers. There are two different groups of traditional healers who have powers beyond a physician's. These are the *inyanga* and the *sangoma.* They serve as prophets, priests, herbalists, and diviners.

The spirit world includes beings that cause misfortune, illness, and trouble. In order to rid someone of these problems, the people turn to the inyanga and the sangoma. They are consulted more often than medical doctors, because they are trusted figures and they are more readily available than physicians.

The inyanga inherits his skills from his male ancestors. He tells the future for an individual by tossing bones and observing the patterns into which they fall. After several tosses, he reads a specific meaning from these patterns.

The sangoma's role is quite different. Sangomas are most often women, and they are called to their profession, often in a

The sangoma may deal in herbal medicine as well as other techniques to help the people under her care.

dream. Once they feel this calling, they apprentice themselves to a practicing sangoma who teaches them the use of herbs and instructs them in how to help people with their problems, both physical and mental. The sangoma is said to be able to "smell out" evil-doers. Medical problems are treated by herbalists who use their knowledge of natural roots and herbs.

Christianity has a large following in Swaziland. It began in the 1840s with the arrival of the first missionaries, who came from South Africa at the invitation of King Mswati II. The Christian group known as the Wesleyans were welcomed as teachers who would bring learning to the people. One of the tasks the missionaries set themselves was to write down the siSwati language. This was undertaken by James Allison. Only after a written language was created could the missionaries begin the job of teaching the Swazis to read and write.

Supplies for traditional medical treatment can be purchased at this open market in Manzini.

The Wesleyans were followed by the Anglicans, who established a mission in 1871, and the Berlin Missionary Society in 1887. There are today a wide variety of church societies in Swaziland. More than half the Swazis consider themselves Christians even though many of them have traditional beliefs as well. Missionaries provided many of the early written accounts of the life and customs of the Swazi people.

MEDICAL HELP ARRIVES

In 1925, Dr. David Hynd, a medical doctor who was also a missionary, arrived from Scotland. Dr. Hynd was given land to build a hospital in the town of Manzini. He combined the practice of religion and medicine. He trained teachers, evangelists, and nurses, who were then sent to the most remote parts of Swaziland. He focused particularly on the problem of leprosy. Largely through his efforts, this devastating disease was mostly eliminated.

More persistent is the problem of malaria, an often fatal disease carried by certain species of mosquitoes. Just as Dr. Hynd focused on leprosy, malaria became the cause taken up by a German physician, Dr. Mastbaum, who came to Swaziland in 1939. He embarked on a program of spraying sleeping huts with DDT. This proved to be very effective against the disease, and the number of deaths in Swaziland decreased dramatically. Today, however, such use has been cut back around the world since DDT was found to have very serious long-term effects on many species of wildlife, especially birds. Malaria remains a serious problem in certain parts of Swaziland, especially in damp regions where mosquitoes breed, as well as in the game reserves.

CATTLE AND BRIDEWEALTH

Traditionally, the central element of rural Swazi life, as in the life of most southern African people, is cattle. The people count wealth in cattle. Each head of cattle has a known cash value and represents a rural Swazi's most important and precious property.

Cattle are not raised to be consumed as meat, the way they are in the United States. The herds play a vital role in Swazi society because cattle are the traditional form of lobola, or bridewealth. The usual amount of lobola is ten head of cattle; one additional animal is given if the daughter is a virgin and so the amount is always stated as eleven cattle. If the girl is the daughter of a chief, the payment is fifteen head of cattle.

Lobola is now usually paid in cash or goods, rather than cattle, since fewer people have access to communal lands where, traditionally, the cattle were grazed. Even the most educated people pay lobola. When Nelson Mandela, now president of South Africa, was preparing to marry off his first daughter, Zenani, lobola had to be discussed. Her intended groom was a Swazi prince. Although Mandela was then still in prison on Robben Island in South Africa, he assigned a good friend to stand in for him during the interview of the groom and especially to negotiate the lobola. The payment of lobola is seen as a way of strengthening the bonds between the families of the bride and groom, giving them a stake in seeing that the marriage is a success.

In modern life, the role of lobola is gradually changing. Parents of more educated young women are demanding higher amounts for lobola. And many feel that the tradition of lobola must continue even though they have moved away from paying lobola with cattle. It shows a respect for the Swazi tradition, a way of retaining important ties within the family.

NGUNI CATTLE

The native cattle of Swaziland are the Nguni, a small and hardy breed particularly well suited to conditions in the country. Its skin is very thick and so it is not bothered with ticks or extremes of heat and cold. It thrives on grasses and other grains that occur naturally in the country, while other breeds of cattle that have been introduced to Swaziland must be fed on imported grain.

Because cattle are needed to pay lobola and play such a central role in the life of rural Swazis, their loss can be devastating. Yet droughts are frequent, unwelcome events in Swaziland. While drought is unavoidable, one of the reasons for the loss of so many head of cattle is that people no longer keep Nguni cattle. They prefer imported cattle, which are large and thus are considered more impressive. During times of drought, grain becomes extremely expensive to import and many people must allow their

The small but hardy Nguni cattle can withstand the droughts that sometimes plague southern Africa. However, there are few large herds left.

cattle to graze on whatever is available. These imported cattle do not do well when they are left to graze.

Today, the only large herd of pure Nguni cattle in Swaziland is on the Mkhaya Nature Reserve. There, in an area with sparse vegetation, one thousand head of Nguni cattle are thriving. As the herd increases, cattle are sold off for their meat, earning money to support the wildlife reserve.

EDUCATION

In the 1940s, only about 6 percent of Swazi children were attending school. Instead, they were taught by their parents and older brothers and sisters, and were educated to take their place in traditional Swazi life. This education focused on practical subjects,

Education for many Swazi children consists only of what is learned at home. This family will teach its children to rethatch the roof on their traditional hut, as well as the different skills needed to repair the roof on the wooden building.

such as how to take care of the cattle and help with the milking, how to build a new home or defend the homestead and the family. Boys were taught to use a spear, to slaughter an animal, and to prepare its skin for use as clothing. Girls were taught to prepare grains for cooking, to make pots and other household items from clay, and to take care of the children. Both boys and girls were prepared to become independent members of their society.

The government does not provide a universal system of education. By the time of independence in 1968, when Swaziland's population was 400,000, 62,000 children were in primary school, but a scant 6,000 were in secondary school. This ratio has scarcely improved through the years. Education is very expensive for the average Swazi, who must pay school fees, buy school uniforms and books, and often even pay for the school to be built. Many of those who do attend school drop out after the first few grades because the costs become overwhelming.

Some primary schools are built, owned, and operated by

This small primary school is located in the small town of Bulembu, near the border with South Africa.

private companies, such as the sugar plantations, often at the specific request of the government. Recently, the sugar companies have added secondary education to their responsibilities.

An academic high school, Sisekelo High School, was built by the Obombo Ranches sugar estate, near the town of Big Bend. The government also asked this company to manage Majombe Primary School, acknowledging that the company was doing a better job of running its schools than was the education ministry.

In an effort to make education more practical, a new high school was opened in 1995 with a special curriculum in electronics and mechanical engineering. A commercial high school teaches children how to be productive farmers. The children pay for seeds, grow crops, sell what they grow, and learn to do the book-keeping for their businesses. Unfortunately, many of the students who manage to graduate from high school discover that there are no jobs to be had.

Students from fifty nations study at the world-famous Waterford Kamhlaba ("The World in Miniature") School on the outskirts of Mbabane. A special fund helps to pay tuition for some Swazi students.

WATERFORD SCHOOL

Ironically, one of the finest secondary schools in Africa is found perched high up on a hillside not far from Mbabane. Called Waterford Kamhlaba, it was started in 1963. At that time, schools in South Africa were rigidly segregated. Many parents, both white and black, wanted their children to have a better and more liberal education than was available at home. They established the school on a farm called Waterford. The siSwati word *kamhlaba* means "the world in miniature," and that is what the school came to represent.

Although it started with just sixteen students living in simple rondavels (bungalows), Waterford grew into an internationally recognized institution, part of the United World College Movement. It now has five hundred students from fifty countries.

During the height of apartheid in South Africa, the children of Nelson Mandela and other political leaders attended Waterford School. Today, some of the grandchildren of those same leaders are among the fifty South Africans attending the school, for although apartheid has ended in South Africa, the quality of education offered to most black students is still not adequate. President Nelson Mandela was recently named the head of the United World College Movement, replacing Prince Charles of Great Britain.

At Waterford, one-quarter of the students are Swazis who, like all the students, must earn a place based on their academic record and a personal interview. Although many of the students come from wealthy families, one-third of them are granted financial aid in order to attend the school. There are usually about two dozen Americans studying at the school, most of them the children of Americans working in Swaziland.

All the students, who range in age from eleven to nineteen, study with the goal of earning an International Baccalaureate diploma, more than equivalent to a high-school diploma. It can earn a graduate up to two years' advanced placement in almost any university.

Above: Women dye Swazi grasses in many bright colors to weave into various objects that sell for both their beauty and their usefulness.
Below: Ngwenya Glassworks recycles glass into useful products using age-old glass-making methods.

Chapter 7

BUSINESS AND INDUSTRY

The development of Swaziland was severely retarded during the colonial era. With the exception of the mining of an asbestos deposit discovered in 1938 in the north at Havelock, the country had virtually no industry. At independence, in 1968, traditional agriculture was the basis of the economy. Even today, more than half the people live by subsistence farming.

Tibiyo takaNgwane, created by King Sobhuza II to buy back the Swazis' land, now oversees virtually the entire economy of Swaziland. Its original funding came from the mining sector. Then it began to acquire shares in the companies that were sprouting in Swaziland.

Today, the organization focuses on agricultural projects, creating housing, and expanding employment opportunities for Swaziland's rapidly growing population. While foreigners are allowed to invest in companies in Swaziland, this has been kept to a minimal level. Local businessmen oppose foreign investment and want the government to allow foreigners in for only a short time. They expect those foreigners to train local people to take over their jobs. This unrealistic expectation is not likely to be met.

The strong desire to keep industry under Swazi control is a

Many Swazis continue to trek into South Africa, remaining for long periods of time to make a living working underground in the gold mines.

result of the country's history, when virtually the entire economy was turned over to outsiders. It is very difficult for a foreigner to obtain employment in Swaziland unless it can be shown that there are no suitably trained Swazis available to fill the position.

TIES WITH SOUTH AFRICA

During the 1980s, Swaziland was swept up in the anti-apartheid movement that focused on cutting off South Africa's business links to the world. Unable to export products with a "Made in South Africa" label, many firms built factories and businesses in Swaziland, which was not affected by these sanctions. With South Africa now a true democracy, however, this active building has halted. Indeed, some companies have closed their factories and moved back to South Africa where transportation and a skilled work force create a better business climate. Swaziland's high tax rate on business—37.5 percent—also discourages investment.

The Swaziland economy remains very closely tied to South Africa's. Although Swaziland has its own currency, called the *lilangeni* (plural form: *emalangeni),* it is fixed at the same rate as the South African rand and is used interchangeably. Both kinds of currency are in circulation throughout Swaziland. When you pay in emalangeni, you may receive your change in either currency.

LOCAL INDUSTRY

In spite of these problems, many firms continue to produce in Swaziland, with their output being sold throughout the southern African region. While government and administration offices are centered in Mbabane, most of the industry and business in Swaziland is conducted in Manzini and the industrial zone called Matsapha, which is found along the main road that connects the two main cities.

Well-known brand names are part of this picture. The Swaziland Bottling Company has the local franchise to bottle Coca-Cola products and Schweppes-brand soft drinks, as well as two popular South African brands, Appletiser and Grapetiser. The company sells two million cases of soft drinks annually in southern Africa. The well-known British candy line, Cadbury, is locally produced in Matsapha at the Cadbury Swaziland plant. Opened in 1989, the plant employs four hundred local people and operates

A South African company brews beer at Matsapha, in the industrial zone (above). A sugar plant near Big Bend (right) employs many people to process sugarcane.

around the clock. It makes use of locally produced sugar, another benefit of being situated in Swaziland.

Although Swaziland is a cotton-growing country, until recently there was no mill in the country to process that cotton. Now the National Textiles mill employs one thousand workers to produce finished yarns as well as fabrics for a variety of markets.

AGRICULTURE

The planting and irrigation of the Usutu Pine Forest began in 1949. Within ten years, half a million pine trees had been planted. In addition, support services such as roads, a township, and an airstrip were created at a new village named Mhlambanyatsi. As the forest began to mature, construction started on a pulp mill in

The Usutu Pine Forest was planted to replace the natural forests that have been destroyed over the years. It covers many thousands of acres and provides wood pulp for many paper products used throughout Africa.

1960 to process the trees into pulp for cardboard, wrapping paper, and other products. Usutu Pulp Company's financing comes from Sappi, the biggest forest products company in Africa. These and other man-made forests cover 4 percent of Swaziland's total land area. These single-species forests stretch for miles in the western part of the country.

In addition to the products made by Usutu Pulp Company, another firm, Swazi Paper Mills, produces tissue paper and other paper products. This company uses recycled wastepaper almost exclusively, making it the most outstanding example of an environmentally friendly operation in Swaziland. The company uses so much recycled paper, it must bring in material from outside sources since Swaziland does not as yet produce enough wastepaper to meet the mill's needs.

Women staff the production line in this Swazican factory at Malkerns where pineapple is being canned.

The easternmost part of Swaziland has the hottest climate of the country. Using irrigation, this area has been turned into a major sugarcane producer. This crop has been so successful it is called "the real Swazi gold." The sugarcane industry was established around Big Bend in 1956 with the construction of the first small sugar mill. Now, three major sugarcane operators, plus several hundred small-scale farmers, grow sugarcane. They usually bring their crops to the large mills for processing. This industry employs some 12,000 people in the fields and mills.

The sugar estates are small cities with their own schools, shopping centers, clinics, and community services. The Simunye estate, for example, employs 3,800 people during the growing season, with a total of 20,000 people (family members making up the total) living on the estate at that time. Local consumption of the sugar mills' output has increased as industries such as Cadbury have moved into Swaziland and provided a local market for their product.

Maize (corn) is grown both commercially and on small family plots because it is the basic foodstuff of the Swazi diet. This woman is pounding maize into flour.

Swaziland's climate is also suitable for cultivation of citrus fruits, especially grapefruits and oranges. These fruits are either sold in fresh form or are processed and canned. On average, four million cartons of citrus fruit are produced each year. A large pineapple plantation is operated by Swaziland Fruit Canners, known as Swazican, which cans the fruits at its factory in Malkerns. Swazican also processes and cans grapefruit and oranges in the form of slices, sections, or juices. Some fruit is also turned into jams and marmalades.

Although these export crops are important money earners for the economy, the most important crop in Swaziland is maize (corn), which is used locally. Maize forms the basis of the Swazi diet. During droughts, which are frequent, local production must be supplemented by imported maize. This imported maize is usually donated outright or bought with grant money supplied by various countries and agencies.

The National Maize Corporation was established in 1985. This government-owned company oversees the production of maize with the goal of making Swaziland self-sufficient in maize growing. While some ears of maize are roasted or boiled and eaten directly off the cob, most maize is ground into meal, which is then cooked into a porridge, the staple food of many people in Swaziland.

MINING

Although southern Africa is rich with precious minerals, Swaziland has few deposits worth mining commercially. Swaziland's biggest mining earnings continue to come from asbestos. Although the country has considerable reserves of coal, production and sales of coal provide much less income than does asbestos. A small-scale diamond mine at Dokolwayo is coming to the end of its productive life since the deposits that remain to be worked are more difficult and expensive to excavate. Stone quarrying makes up the fourth area of mining. This stone is used by the local construction industry, especially in road building. Although there are gold deposits, these have never been exploited and may not be large enough to justify the large-scale mining structure required to mine gold.

An ancient iron ore mine in the Ngwenya Mountains, said to be the oldest in the world, is open to the public as a tourist attraction. Its modern commercial production ended in 1978. The

Swaziland's minerals have not been intensively mined. This old iron mine (left) provided iron for Japan's steel for many years but is now closed. The Havelock Asbestos mine, the oldest working mine in Swaziland, is now a tourist attraction. The power station is shown at right.

country's railway system started at the mine in order to transport the ore to the Indian Ocean port of Maputo in Mozambique.

TRADITIONAL CRAFTS

For most Swazis, especially the women, handicrafts offer a way to earn money, usually without leaving home and children. Since independence, the crafts movement has grown enormously and now provides employment for thousands of women. Using local materials for the most part, and some of the traditional skills of the Swazi culture, along with both modern materials and newly acquired skills, this hands-on industry produces a wide variety of useful and decorative items.

The ability to create a business with enough financing to make materials available on a regular basis, to keep a flow of products in and out of stock, and to design products that attract buyers, often require skills not well developed in Swaziland. For that reason, many of the craft businesses in Swaziland are directed by Europeans, some of whom have lived in the country for more than twenty years. They have taken such traditional Swazi crafts as pottery making and basket weaving and applied them to making products that have great appeal to tourists as well as to people living in southern Africa. Most of the crafts centers and workshops are concentrated around Mbabane.

More than twenty years ago, Jennie Thorn arrived in Swaziland from England and discovered that she could not practice her profession of nursing because outsiders were not allowed to take jobs in the country. Looking for a way to make money and to give employment to rural women, she turned to traditional crafts. While there was no sense of crafts as an industry, the skills were readily available.

Jennie and her husband began to develop a variety of crafts in a business called Tishweshwe, located near the Royal Kraal, halfway between Mbabane and Manzini. Today, Tishweshwe sells the work of hundreds of craftspeople including basketry, pottery, mohair tapestries, leatherwork, and jewelry. The name *Tishweshwe* means "of the people" and was used to describe the cloth that was first brought in by the missionaries. When they converted people to Christianity, one of the first requirements was to clothe them. The cloth they brought was worn only by the Africans.

Leaving Tishweshwe in the early 1990s, Jennie Thorn opened her own business, called Gone Rural. She specializes in pottery and products made from the local grass called *lutindzi*. Women

Special local grasses are dyed by women who then make them into many different craft products (left). Bright fabrics, using traditional Swazi designs, are sold to both residents and visitors (above).

have been braiding this grass for traditional use as roofing and mats for the home. It was just a few steps from that use to finding products they could make using the same skills but that would be attractive to outsiders. She encourages the women to locate and harvest the wild grasses that grow in the mountainous areas, tucked in rocky crags.

The grass is dyed behind the workshop and spread out on mats to dry. When a woman brings in a bundle of grass, it is exchanged for a bundle that has been dyed in attractive and fashionable colors. She takes this bundle home and weaves placemats, small baskets, and many other household products. When she returns with the finished goods, she brings another bundle of grass to exchange. In this way, a woman can get started and can earn money immediately.

Although it seems easy to do, working with the supple grass

Skilled pottery makers sell their pots along the roadside. Their beehive hut tempts visitors to stop and purchase.

requires a very deft hand to produce a uniform braid and a finely finished product. Gone Rural's workers now produce more crafts than can be sold in Swaziland, and the firm has taken on an agent who markets their products in South Africa. It is estimated that as many as half the women in Swaziland are doing some kind of craft work that enables them to earn money to pay school fees and buy school uniforms and books for their children.

The traditional clay pot made by Swazi women enjoys great favor with local buyers. Because the pots are quite heavy, only the smallest sizes are easily carried home by visitors. In Swazi culture, the small pot, called *ludzino,* was used as an individual beer pot. This pot, which is really a cup without handles, has been adapted to other uses. At Gone Rural, some of these pots are filled with scented candles. Small decorative beads are pressed into the clay before it is baked. Each potter makes these items at home, in a small oven heated by a wood fire.

Mantenga Craft Center lies between Mbabane and Manzini, where it can draw many visitors to the work of talented craftspeople.

At the Mantenga Craft Center, located just a few kilometers off the main road that connects Swaziland's cities, a craft village has been created by Pauline Woodall. The whole range of crafts made in Swaziland—pottery, weaving, basketry, clothing, sculpture, glass, leather, silk screen printing, and more—are shown and sold here in different shops. The shops are arranged along a little walkway that encourages visitors to browse and visit. Craftsmakers are also present, displaying their skills as they produce goods. Sisal baskets, a traditional Swazi craft, are featured at

Mantenga in sizes ranging from tiny to extra large. Sisal, a natural plant material, is traditionally used for mats and roofing.

Mantenga, which was started in 1974, offers crafts made by individuals as well as the work of small manufacturers. The workshops and showrooms operate as a nonprofit organization. All the profits are directed toward the purchase of raw materials and training to make women self-sufficient.

CONTEMPORARY CRAFTS

The skillful hands of Swazi men and women have also been directed to non-traditional materials and methods, resulting in beautiful, useful, and decorative work. One of the oldest firms is Ngwenya Glass, located near the Ngwenya-South Africa border post. *Ngwenya* means "crocodile." Once plentiful in this area, crocodiles have become the symbol of the company.

In the 1970s, a team of Swedish glassblowers trained Swazis in this ancient craft. The firm specializes in glassware for the table as well as small decorative animal figures. What sets Ngwenya Glass apart, however, is that it uses recycled glass exclusively. The company gets this glass from many sources including school-children, who are encouraged to pick up discarded glass bottles, wash them, and bring them to collecting centers at their schools. The schoolchildren use the money they receive for the glass for special activities at school. They also like the idea that a portion of the profits from Ngwenya Glass are donated to the international Save the Rhino Fund.

The glassblowing is carried out in the traditional manner seen in glassworks around the world. The men work in teams, with

A woodcarver's fine statues are exhibited in a stand near the main road in the Ezulwini Valley.

one man inserting a hollow metal tube into the oven where the glass is melted, picking up a "gob" on the end of the tube, and then blowing gently into the tube to begin the shaping process. He hands this over to another worker who shapes the glass with wooden tools, while turning it constantly. Meanwhile the glass is cooling and hardening, so the shaping must be done quickly. Another worker takes the finished piece, still on the rod, and carries it to the annealing oven where the temperature is first raised and then slowly lowered. If this were not done, the glass would be very brittle and would shatter.

Drinking glasses are also made at the factory. These are finished by women who polish the rims to a smooth finish on big grinding tables.

TAPESTRIES

Weaving is another skill known around the world. At Endlotane Studios/Phumalanga Tapestries, this traditional skill has been elevated to a fine art. Albert Christoph Reck, who came

Some very talented women have learned the new craft of creating paintings in fine wool tapestries that sell around the world.

to Swaziland in the mid-1970s, is an artist who creates paintings that are turned into tapestries.

The work begins with mohair, some of it from the workshop's own goats. This mohair, a very fine and soft wool, is spun into yarn and then dyed in many different shades. The firm employs forty-five to fifty women to do the weaving. These women are trained by Reck and his wife, Marie-Louise. It takes about a year for a weaver to learn enough to be productive.

Each woman works on a loom in front of the painting she is weaving. It takes a good deal of artistic interpretation to turn the painted image into the woven tapestry, and the women take great pride in their work. One woman requires about two months to produce a tapestry that measures about 4 by 6 feet (1.2 by 1.8 meters). Themes used in the tapestries are taken from the natural environment as well as from ancient rock paintings originally created by the San, or Bushmen, who once inhabited the region.

Special orders form an important part of the firm's output. King Mswati ordered a tapestry that he presented in person to the Martin Luther King, Jr., Center in Atlanta, Georgia. One spectacular commission came as the result of a worldwide competition. This firm won the commission to create a huge tapestry, measuring 7,320 square feet (680 square meters) for the airport in Tampa, Florida. Thirteen Swazi weavers traveled to the United States to do the work and lived there for two years until the tapestry was completed.

ARTIST AT WORK

In addition to the craftsmakers, Swaziland also has fine artists. Their work is shown in galleries such as Ndglise Gallery, located near the shopping plaza in Mbabane. One of the best artists in Swaziland is Austin Hleza, a sculptor and print maker. Hleza makes lino prints, cutting designs into linoleum and then printing them on paper or cloth. His subjects are the scenes he sees all around him, including a bus station as well as a scene showing Sibhaca dancers—the traditional Swazi dance.

For his fine pottery, he uses black clay found near Swazican. This clay enables him to fire his pieces at a higher temperature, resulting in a finer product. Hleza has built his own kiln not far from the Ngwenya Glassworks. Hleza has been a guest artist at the Waterford School where he shows the students in an art class how to make vases and bowls. By working with these international students, he helps bring many worlds together.

Above: The Royal Swazi Sun is Swaziland's best known hotel.
Left: At Mkhaya Nature Reserve, skulls from rhinoceros killed by poachers reveal the devastating loss of animals.
Below: Actors perform in an open-air theater.

Chapter 8

BUILDING TOWARD THE FUTURE

Many developing countries are turning to tourism to add to their economic activity. Swaziland's geographic situation has given it an unusual advantage in the highly competitive world of tourism. During the apartheid years in South Africa, visitors found it pleasant to vacation across the border in Swaziland where race was not an issue. As a result, Swaziland's tourist facilities are better than would ordinarily have been true of such a small country. Swaziland's resorts and one casino provide employment opportunities for the local people. These top-ranked facilities require hundreds of well-trained staff members filling a variety of positions. Swazis are found in virtually every job category. Several members of the royal family work in this industry.

Swaziland's best-known resort is the Royal Swazi Sun Hotel and Casino, located in the Ezulwini Valley not far from Mbabane. *Ezulwini* means "valley of heaven." Many people come to know Swaziland when they attend a convention there. The facilities include an auditorium that seats 600 people. Local Swazi products are used throughout the complex wherever possible. The casino, located in a separate building next to the hotel, employs Swazi women as croupiers and dealers.

Executioner's Rock is a feature of the beautiful Ezulwini Valley (left). An employee of one of the hotels in the valley (above) became Miss Swaziland and competed in the Miss World competition in London.

When Nyamalele Ndlovu was working as a croupier at the Royal Swazi Sun in 1978, she entered the Miss Swaziland contest and was crowned in a dramatic evening ceremony. She represented Swaziland in London at the Miss World contest later that year. Her life as an educated, modern Swazi woman encompasses working and shopping in Mbabane, yet she also embraces traditional Swazi culture. She took part in the Reed Dance each year for five years after she turned twelve.

Before the end of apartheid in South Africa, the Royal Swazi Sun convention center was one of the few places in the region where multiracial business groups could meet. The casino also drew people from South Africa, where games of chance were illegal. However, when Sun City, a gambling center, was built in South Africa, Swaziland lost much of the casino business. They made up for that loss with the convention center.

Two other large hotels, located along the main road, are the Ezulwini Sun Hotel and the Lugogo Sun. All are part of the same hotel group as the Royal Swazi Sun.

WILDLIFE RESERVES

As is fitting for a small country, Swaziland's wildlife reserves are also small. But their small size allows for an intimate view of wildlife. The country is dotted with game parks: Malolotja Natural Reserve, Mlilwane Wildlife Sanctuary, Hlane Game Reserve, Mlawula Nature Reserve, and Mkhaya Nature Reserve. All were originally supported by King Sobhuza II who had a great love of the wild creatures.

Each reserve offers something different in the kind of terrain and the wildlife. All are being nurtured, often in the face of serious threats from poachers and farmers who want grazing land. It is the job of the wildlife conservationists to show that preserving wildlife can be more profitable than destroying it. One of the champions of Swaziland's wildlife is Ted Reilly who almost single-handedly created and nurtured the Mkhaya Nature Reserve and Mlilwane Wildlife Sanctuary.

There was virtually no wildlife left in Swaziland by the beginning of the twentieth century because of overhunting by Europeans. Also the region was hit by rinderpest, a plague that virtually destroyed Swaziland's entire populations of buffalo, giraffe, sable antelope, impala, and hartebeest. There used to be thousands of impala in Swaziland. Even the vultures deserted Swaziland because there was nothing left for them to feed on. The wildlife began to return, especially the wildebeest, which moved in from neighboring countries. However, it was once more hunted out of existence by Europeans who saw these creatures as pests that interfered with their farming and cattle raising.

Mlilwane Wildlife Sanctuary was created out of a wasteland

Visitors to Mlilwane Wildlife Sanctuary can ride horseback to view the
natural setting (left). The sanctuary features the famous Hippo Pool (right),
where a brave warthog faces off with a cumbersome hippo.

that was the result of overhunting and intensive farming. Even
the birds had disappeared. Ted Reilly and his family set
themselves the task of turning their own farming estate into a
wildlife sanctuary. After they fenced off the park's boundaries,
they began to introduce wildlife, one animal at a time. Then a rest
camp was created out of simple, local materials.

The central attraction of Mlilwane is the Hippo Pool. Here,
hippopotamuses and crocodiles abound. The hippos emerge
ponderously from the pool every afternoon when cereal is put out.
The cereal was meant to attract birds, but the hippos soon decided
to take advantage of this free meal. This allows visitors a close
look at this remarkable animal that spends most of its time
submerged in water up to its eyes. All that separates the hippos

A white rhino mother and baby may be seen at Mkhaya Nature Reserve. The reserve is working to preserve this rare species, which is subject to massive poaching for its valuable horn.

from people is a low stone wall. A special feature of game viewing at Mlilwane is that visitors can travel by horseback along mountain trails that are not accessible by vehicle.

The most remarkable wildlife conservation story in Swaziland is that of Mkhaya Nature Reserve, where the extremely endangered rhinoceros may be seen. The name *Mkhaya* is taken from the distinctive knobberry tree, the most plentiful tree in the reserve.

It is due to the efforts of Ted Reilly that the rhinos at Mkhaya exist. He began to acquire both species of rhino, black and white, in 1987. Funds had to be secured for the purchase of each animal. They are usually sold in breeding groups of five animals at a cost of $250,000 for the group.

But rhinos are more vulnerable to poaching than any other

animal on the African continent. Their horn is valued by people in Asia, who believe it has medicinal properties. In order to get the horn, poachers shoot the animal with automatic weapons, cut out the horn, and then leave the carcass to rot. The obsessive desire for rhino horn has very nearly wiped out the entire species.

Poachers invaded Mkhaya between 1988 and 1992, killing almost all the rhinos that had been brought there. The skulls of dozens of these animals are stacked up at the entrance to the reserve. It is a sobering sight and makes viewing the live animals from close up even more special.

You can actually touch the ostriches at Mkhaya. These curious birds—the world's largest—come right up to the game ranger's vehicle in which visitors tour the reserve. They come close enough to have their feathers stroked.

Elephants were also reintroduced to the game parks of Swaziland after having been hunted out entirely by the 1950s. A donation of eight animals was made by the National Parks Board of South Africa, while ten others were sold to Swaziland at a special price. The elephant is the symbol of the queen mother in Swaziland, and it holds a special place in Swazi cultural tradition.

In spite of official support from the Kingdom, the only parks in Swaziland that are economical are those that operate without government funds. These are Mlilwane, Mkhaya, and Hlane Royal National Park. Fencing costs, a crucial element in keeping poachers out and wildlife in, have been met by grants from the European Union. At Hlane, this resulted in the reintroduction of lions, brought in from South Africa's Kruger National Park. The lion is the symbol of the king, so the return of the lion had great significance in Swaziland.

Mbabane, the capital city of Swaziland, was first established in 1902, when British officials decided its western location was healthier than Manzini. Today its focus is the Mall. Its residents welcome the new fast-food restaurants.

CITIES

The principal cities in Swaziland are Mbabane and Manzini. The name of the capital, *Mbabane,* means "something sharp and bitter." The population is estimated at nearly 50,000 and growing rapidly. It lies in the westernmost part of the country, not far from the border post of Ngwenya. Mbabane lies nestled within a range

This supermarket is in Manzini, which was originally established as Bremersdorp. It is the center of the country's industrial region.

of hills and has a small-town feeling. A shopping center forms the central attraction.

Manzini, now connected to Mbabane by a modern road, lies nearly in the center of the country. The station for the railroad line linking the country to Maputo in Mozambique and to Durban and Richards Bay in South Africa is found here. At one time, Manzini, then known as Bremersdorp, was the capital city. The town was founded in 1892. Manzini is the central supply district for the industrial and manufacturing zone of Matsapha, which lies just outside the town.

Swaziland is no exception to the popularity of soccer, or football, in Africa. This game (left) is being played at Piggs Peak. An international swim meet (right) was held in Swaziland in 1995.

SPORTS

Swimming is one of the sports that has become very popular among schoolchildren who have access to a swimming pool. In 1995, Swaziland was chosen as the site for an international swim meet featuring teams from the neighboring countries of Zimbabwe, Botswana, and South Africa. The teams, which included students from primary school through high school, met at an Mbabane primary school and enjoyed several days of competition. Swaziland's team did very well, but they lost first place to the team from the Transvaal province of South Africa.

LOOKING AHEAD TO CHANGE

As the twenty-first century begins, African nations like Swaziland must find a way to retain their traditions while adapting to the demands of modern life. King Mswati III recognizes that it is no longer appropriate for him to take dozens of wives and have hundreds of children as his father did. He has had to stand up to the more conservative advisors who want him to follow tradition.

Swaziland is one of only three African nations ruled by a king. The other two are Morocco and Lesotho. In other African nations, there are kings who rule only over the cultural life of their people. The *kabaka* of the Baganda people was recently reinstated in Uganda, and in Zambia, the king of the Lozi people continues to play an important role in his people's lives. However, these two countries are ultimately ruled by presidents.

Swaziland has been surrounded by dramatic change in the last few years. The end of apartheid in South Africa and the opening up of the South African economy have already brought about the shift of some manufacturing businesses as well as tourism from Swaziland. The new openness of the South African political system offers a compelling contrast to Swaziland's. While dissent, especially on the part of Swazi university students, has been suppressed, it continues to grow. They have seen protest and pressure work elsewhere.

On September 23, 1995, King Mswati III announced that a group would be formed to develop a new constitution or to revive the constitution that was suspended by King Sobhuza II in 1973. Without a written constitution, there is no way to make people accountable for their actions. This is an important step for King Mswati and the people of Swaziland. This time, the constitutional process was not done in secret, as it had been in 1978 under the former king.

Since the colonial powers entered southern Africa, the Swazi people have worked toward getting their own land back.

On Swaziland's eastern border lies Mozambique. During that country's long civil war, Swaziland offered refuge to more than 20,000 people. Even though many of them lived in refugee camps, they had an impact on the country. And now they, too, have returned to a country where positive changes are taking place. Maputo, the capital of Mozambique, is little more than an hour's drive from parts of Swaziland and only four hours from Mbabane.

LONGING FOR LAND

Although the borders of Swaziland were fixed many years ago, many Swazis still feel a sense of loss for the land that was once considered part of the kingdom. The principal lost area, known as KaNgwane, lies directly to the west of Swaziland and is now part of South Africa. During the apartheid years, this was designated by South Africa as the Swazi homeland, a place where the Swazi people of South Africa were supposed to live. Swazi officials must often deal with the Swazi people who live in KaNgwane and who traditionally consider themselves to be subjects of the Swazi king, not citizens of South Africa.

Some Swazis harbored the dream that someday they would reclaim KaNgwane, and this dream nearly came true. Just before he died, Sobhuza was negotiating a deal in which South Africa would give up a strip of KaNgwane, on Swaziland's northern border, as well as a vital corridor that would allow Swaziland access to the Indian Ocean, right through KwaZulu, the traditional homeland of the Zulu people. Swaziland's part of the bargain was to actively put down the activities of the black South Africans who were fighting to free their country from white rule. However, the people of the two areas, especially those who were ruled by Zulu Chief Minister Buthelezi, were vehemently against the plan, and the deal never went through.

According to the most recent census, there are 950,000 Swazis living in South Africa, including those who live in urban areas and in KaNgwane. That is more than the number of Swazis living in Swaziland, which is estimated at 800,000.

RELATIONS WITH THE WORLD

Swaziland's most important relations in Europe are with Great Britain, its former colonial ruler. It is part of the Commonwealth group of nations, all having ties to Great Britain. Although the United States has been an important donor of aid to Swaziland,

King Mswati III (left) meets with South Africa's president Nelson Mandela.

this aid is diminishing rapidly because the U.S. Congress is actively cutting foreign aid allotments. The Peace Corps program in Swaziland was being phased out in 1996.

Swaziland's most important foreign relationship is with South Africa, its neighbor. South Africa and Swaziland share many problems, particularly the growing rate of crime. King Mswati has met with South African president Nelson Mandela, who pressed the king to lead his country in a more democratic fashion. But the king defends his style of leadership. When he came to the United States to take part in the Fiftieth Anniversary celebration of the United Nations, he addressed the general assembly as one of the youngest leaders in the world. He looked very far ahead saying, "If God is willing, I may be one of the very few who will be present when we commemorate our organization's centenary celebrations, in the year 2045."

There is no question about the continuation of the monarchy,

The long reign of King Sobhuza II, memorialized in this beautiful monument, left the Swazi people ready to begin to work toward change in their relationship to the monarchy.

but there is a strong desire to have a more democratic nation with a constitutional monarch. In the midst of the powerful changes taking place in South Africa, Swaziland needs a strong, thoughtful leader who can find a role for this small, proud nation.

THE PRICE OF ROYALTY

Whether a country is a democracy or a monarchy, it costs money to run the government. The question for many people is whether Swaziland's monarchy costs too much money. Although it is said that only the king and the queen mother are supported directly from the national budget, there are dozens, even hundreds, of members of the royal family who live in greater comfort than most Swazi citizens. And it is very difficult to know

A demonstration at Somhlolo National Stadium was organized for King Mswati's birthday. Though its character may change, the monarchy is important to most Swazis.

who is really a prince or princess and who is just pretending.

One of the costs of royalty is the power of the Dlamini family, the most important in Swaziland. They hold many of the positions of power in the government and in business. The name is so common, it is like Jones or Smith in the United States. When elections for Parliament were held in 1993, Michael Dlamini was one of the successful candidates. Just twenty-two years old, he ran against six older, richer, and better-known men. He believes he won because he talked about the need for laws to protect those in need. But it is likely that people voted for him because they believed a Dlamini would wield more power.

The most visible expense for the nation, however, is King Mswati. The king's birthday is a national holiday celebrated in extravagant fashion. In 1995, 5,550 guests were invited to the king's birthday party. The provisions for the party included sixty large animals, each weighing 500 pounds (226.8 kilograms). Yet in that same year, a persistent drought left many people without enough food to eat. When the king traveled to the United Nations in New York that year, there were more than thirty people in his party, many more than President Nelson Mandela had with him for the same occasion.

Much of the cost of supporting the royal family comes from its shares in the businesses of the nation, but people would rather see that money used for such basics as building schools, providing a free education for all Swazi children, and building more health clinics and better hospitals. With the changes in South Africa, there is a fear that more and more businesses will leave Swaziland. Should that happen, the amount of money available to spend on services will shrink even as the number of Swazis continues to grow. Once, Swaziland felt that it was ahead of the other countries in the region. Now, with the changes in South Africa and Mozambique, the people realize they have been left behind in the regional move toward economic growth and political stability.

THE FUTURE

While there is no question that Swaziland will continue to be a nation headed by a king, the desire to have a more democratic nation within that monarchy will only grow stronger. The decision to allow a new constitution to be written gives Swaziland the appearance of a country more in step with the rest of southern Africa. It gives the Swazi people a sense that there are laws

Even heavy rain did not keep these street vendors from demonstrating against government policies in 1995. This rare protest may be just the beginning of Swazi citizens playing a greater role in decision-making in Swaziland.

governing their lives and that these laws are known to all. In July 1996, King Mswati III appointed Barnabas Sibusiso Dlamini as the country's new prime minister.

Swaziland's borders with South Africa, the most powerful nation in southern Africa, are secure; it has no need to defend itself against invasion. There are no freedom fighters from neighboring countries asking for refuge within its borders. Swaziland no longer acts as a transit point for goods coming from South Africa, as it did during the apartheid years. The dramatic shift to black majority rule in South Africa and the end of the long war in Mozambique ensure a continuing peaceful future for Swaziland.

Swaziland will always find its essence as a nation through its own traditions. They enable Swaziland to maintain an identity that is unique in the region and guarantee the nation a special place in the ever-changing continent of Africa.

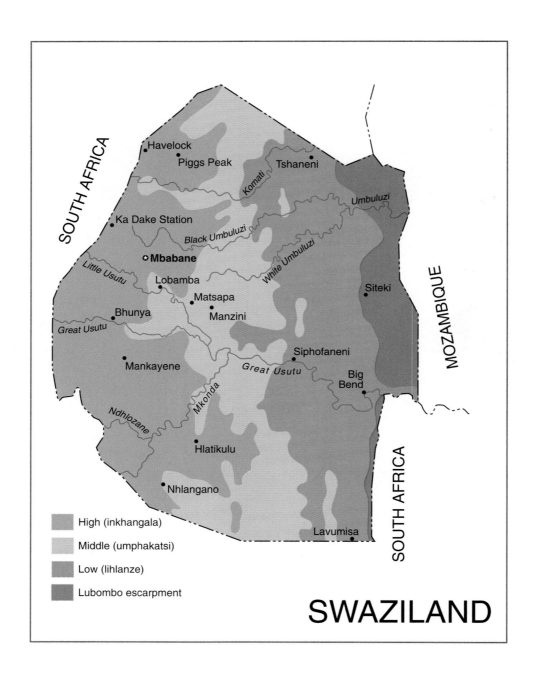

SWAZILAND

High (inkhangala)
Middle (umphakatsi)
Low (lihlanze)
Lubombo escarpment

MINI-FACTS AT A GLANCE

GENERAL INFORMATION

Official Name: Umbuso weSwatini (in siSwati); Kingdom of Swaziland (English).

Capital: Mbabane is the administrative capital and Lobamba is the royal and legislative capital.

Government: Swaziland is a constitutional monarchy. The constitution vests supreme executive, legislative, and judicial powers in the hereditary king, known as *ngwenyama* (the "Lion"), who governs the country with the assistance of an appointed cabinet. There are two houses of Parliament—the Upper House (Senate) and the.House of Assembly. The Parliament is restricted to debating government proposals and advising the king. The judiciary is headed by a chief justice and consists of a high court with six subordinate courts. For administrative purposes, the country is divided into four districts.

Religion: More than 50 percent of the Swazi people consider themselves to be Christians, although they follow traditional beliefs as well. Swazis believe strongly in a spirit world that is closely connected with the everyday world.

Ethnic Composition: The Swazi make up the largest indigenous African population group, consisting of more than 70 clans; the Dlamini, the royal clan, is dominant. Swazi form about 85 percent of the population, followed by Zulu, 10 percent; Tsonga, 3 percent; and others (Indians, Pakistanis, Portuguese), 2 percent.

Language: Both siSwati and English are official languages. English is taught in schools and both languages are used in conducting business. SiSwati language belongs to the Benue-Congo group of the Niger-Congo languages.

National Flag: The Swazi flag has two blue horizontal stripes at top and bottom; two narrow yellow stripes separate the blue stripes from a wide crimson stripe in the center. On this crimson stripe is a black and white Swazi shield superimposed on two spears and a staff, all lying horizontally. Blue signifies peace; yellow, natural resources; and crimson, past battles.

National Emblem: A bright blue outer shield has an oval black and white inner shield, flanked by a lion (representing the king) and an elephant (representing the queen mother). A headdress of otter skin and bird feathers is at the top of the emblem, and the national motto, "We are the Fortress," is engraved on a scroll at the bottom of the emblem.

National Calendar: Gregorian.

National Anthem: "O Lord our God, bestower of the blessings upon the Swazi."

Money: The national currency is called the *lilangeni* (plural form is *emalangeni).* It is fixed at the same rate as the South African rand with which it is used interchangeably. In 1996, one U.S. dollar was worth more than four emalangeni.

Membership in International Organizations: African, Caribbean and Pacific States (ACP); African Development Bank (AfDB); the Commonwealth; International Monetary Fund (IMF); Organization of African Unity (OAU); Southern African Development Coordination Community (SADCC); Southern African Customs Union; United Nations (UN).

Weights and Measures: The metric system is used.

Population: 1996 estimates 931,500, with a density of 138 persons per sq. mi. (53 persons per sq. km). 34 percent of the people live in cities and 66 percent live in rural areas.

Cities:

Manzini 71,871
Mbabane 52,780
Piggs Peak 4,404
Big Bend 3,990
Siteki 3,267

(Figures based on unofficial 1996 estimates)

GEOGRAPHY

Border: South Africa forms the northern, southern, and western boundaries, and Mozambique forms the eastern boundary.

Coastline: Swaziland is a small landlocked country with no coastline.

Land: In spite of its small size, Swaziland's geography is varied and ranges from high mountains to low-lying farmlands. The land can be divided into four topographical regions from west to east. The mountains (called the high belt, or veld), covering 30 percent of the total land area in the westernmost region, are continuations of the Drakensberg Range; to the east lies the farmland region (middle belt), covering 28 percent of total land with the highest concentration of population; farther east, a dry and hot belt of flat, rolling plains (low belt) covers 33 percent of land; and lastly the sharply rising Lubombo escarpment in the easternmost part covers 9 percent of land and separates Swaziland from Mozambique.

Highest Point: Mount Emlembe, 6,109 ft. (1,862 m).

Lowest Point: 70 ft. (21 m) above sea level.

Rivers: Swaziland is one of the best-watered countries in southern Africa. The Komati, Lomati, Pongola, Mkhondvo, Great Usutu, and Little Usutu are the major perennial rivers flowing eastward into Mozambique, and eventually emptying into the Indian Ocean. These rivers have great hydroelectric potential and provide irrigation to large-scale fruit and sugarcane estates.

Forests: Less than 8 percent of the land is covered by forests, out of which some 5 percent is manmade pine and eucalyptus forest. Under the Usutu Pine Forest Plan, about half a million pine trees have been planted within ten years, providing wood pulp for the local paper industry.

Wildlife: Country's original wildlife of buffalo, kudu, giraffe, impala, zebra, sable antelope, ostrich, elephants, hippopotamus, crocodiles, rhinoceros, wildebeest, and hartebeest was greatly reduced by hunting, poaching, and rinderpest disease. There was virtually no wildlife left in the country by the beginning of the twentieth century. Due to the efforts of wildlife conservationists, nature reserves and parks were established where remaining wildlife is protected. Bird life includes herons, stork, and ibis.

Swaziland has several wildlife reserves including Malolotja Natural Reserve, Mlilwane Wildlife Sanctuary, Hlane Game Reserve, Mlawula Nature Reserve, and Mkhaya Nature Reserve. Each of these reserves offers something different in the kind of terrain and in the wildlife. Fencing to keep poachers out is paid for mostly by grants from the European Union.

Climate: Swaziland's climate varies from subtropical in the east to temperate in the hilly west. Mean annual temperatures are 59° F. (15° C) in the west and 72° F. (22° C) in the east. Temperatures range from as low as 27° F. (-3° C) in winter in the highlands to as high as 108° F. (42° C) in summer in the lowlands. Rainfall is concentrated in the summer months from October to March and varies from 100 in. (250 cm) in the west to 35 in. (85 cm) in the east.

Greatest Distance: North to South: 120 mi. (193 km).

East to West: 90 mi. (140 km).

Area: 6,704 sq. mi. (17,364 sq. km).

ECONOMY AND INDUSTRY

Agriculture: More than half of the population depends on subsistence agriculture. Clan chiefs allocate land for farming. Maize (corn), rice, potato, and sweet potato are the chief subsistence crops, while sugarcane, tobacco, and cotton are the chief cash crops. Grapefruits and oranges, the main citrus crops, are either sold fresh or processed and canned. Europeans own almost one-half the country's land where they operate large plantations. Some large European sugarcane estates support 20,000 people and provide schools, shopping centers, and clinics.

Cattle: Cattle are the central element in Swazi life, representing a rural Swazi's most important and precious property. They are not raised and kept as a source of meat, but they are the traditional form of bridewealth. The small and hardy Nguni are the native cattle of Swaziland. This bovine's skin is very thick and so it is not bothered with ticks and heat or cold. It survives on the grasses and grains that occur naturally in the country. An increasing number of Swazis are keeping imported cattle, which must eat imported grains rather than local grasses. This fact prevents them from surviving drought as well as Nguni.

Mining: Swaziland's mineral deposits include coal, asbestos, stone, barite (from which barium is taken), kaolin (clay for making pottery), and pyrophyllite. The gold deposits have not been exploited because the quantity is too small. The diamond mine at Dokolwayo is almost exhausted and is no longer being worked. The iron mine near Ngwenga is open only as a tourist attraction as production has ceased.

Manufacturing: Foreign investment in industry and manufacturing is allowed but is kept to a minimal level. Most of the industries and manufacturing are centered in Manzini and at the industrial zone of Matsapha. The Swaziland Bottling Company bottles Coca-Cola products, Schweppes-brand soft drinks, and some other brands. The well-known candy line, Cadbury, is produced in Matsapha. The National Textiles Mill produces yarns and fabrics.

The Usutu Pulp mill processes pine trees into pulp for cardboard, wrapping paper, and other products. The Swazi Paper mills produce tissue paper and other paper products exclusively from recycled paper. Swaziland Fruit Canners process citrus fruits in the form of slices, sections, juices, jams, and marmalades. Other manufactured items are textiles, cement, agricultural machinery, fertilizer, food products, footwear, and electronic equipment. Swaziland's manufacturing sector is larger than that of most African countries.

Transportation: In 1993 there were 199 mi. (320 km) of railroads used only for cargo as they provide the major transport link for imports and exports. They connect Swaziland with the South African ports of Richards Bay, Durban, and Komatipoort, and the Mozambique port of Maputo. Railways are not used for passenger traffic. Buses are the primary mode of transportation for Swazis. Most villages or kraals are connected by footpaths. The total length of roads is about 1,740 mi. (2.800 km), of which a third are paved. The international airport is at Matsapha, near Manzini. Royal Swazi National Airways is the national airline; Air Swazi Cargo and African International Airways (AIA) operate cargo services.

Communication: Television and radio are state-owned. Color transmission television broadcasts seven hours daily in English. There are three daily newspapers, all in English. In the early 1990s, there was one radio receiver per 13 persons, one television set per 65 persons, and one telephone per 40 persons.

Trade: Chief imports are machinery and transport equipment, minerals, beverages and tobacco, chemicals, petroleum, and food items. Major import sources are South Africa, United Kingdom, Singapore, Hong Kong, Denmark, and the Netherlands. Chief export items are sugar, wood and wood products, canned fruits, diamonds, and asbestos. Major export destinations are South Africa, the United States, United Kingdom, Mozambique, South Korea, and Zimbabwe.

EVERYDAY LIFE

Health: Medical facilities in general are better in Swaziland than other African countries as medical services are provided by the government, missions, industrial estates, and private physicians. Major health problems include infectious intestinal diseases, tuberculosis, malnutrition, and respiratory diseases. Malaria is still a serious problem, especially in damp regions and game reserves. Health conditions are generally poor, as is indicated by a low life expectancy of 56 years for males and 60 years for females. The infant-mortality rate at 73 per 1,000 is high. In the early 1990s, there were about 9,300 persons per physician and about 400 persons per hospital bed. More than 80 percent of Swazis believe in healing by traditional healers and avoid going to a doctor or a hospital. Traditional healers, *sangoma,* are mostly women trained in the use of herbs and natural roots. They help people with mental and physical problems.

Education: Education is not compulsory, but government-funded schools are available throughout the country. The education system consists of seven years of primary school and five years of secondary school. Since the government does not provide a universal system of education, many schools are run by missions. There are many private schools. Education is not free. It is very expensive for an average Swazi family who pays fees, buys uniforms and books, and often pays for the building of the schools. Many private companies have their own primary schools for children of the employees on their estates.

There are very few high schools. One of the finest secondary schools in Africa is the Waterford Kamhlaba near Mbabane. It is an internationally recognized institution with about five hundred students from fifty countries. The University of Swaziland is at Matsapha with campuses at Luyengo and Kwaluseni. There are three teacher-training colleges and eight vocational institutions. In the late 1980s, the literacy rate was about 67 percent.

Culture: The two most important ceremonies of the Swazi people are the Reed Dance and the Ncwala, or first fruits. The Reed Dance, or *umhlanga*, is a week-long series of events focused on the unmarried girls of the kingdom. The month-long Ncwala, or the ceremony of the first fruits, has sacred qualities and is closely tied to the Swazi king. This time of great joy marks the beginning of the harvest season. All important national ceremonies are held at Lobamba, the royal village.

Holidays:

> New Year's Day, January 1
> Commonwealth Day, second Monday in March
> National Flag Day, April 25
> King Sobhuza II's birthday, July 22
> Reed Dance, last Monday in August
> Independence Day, September 6
> United Nations Day, October 24
> Christmas, December 25

Movable religious holidays are Good Friday, Holy Saturday, Easter Monday, and Ncwala (National) Ceremony.

Society: The clan chiefs are the law in Swazi villages and people live under their close guidance. Many of the chiefs are members of the royal family. The chief's position is passed down from father to son. Every event in the *kraal* (homestead) is reported to the chief, and he is consulted about every aspect of daily life. An extended family group lives under a headman (chief) and his mother, the chief woman. Communal huts are built around the cattle pen where animals are kept at night. A Swazi man can have more than one wife, and each wife gets her own hut and a small piece of land. Each kraal has a granary pit to store the food distributed by the headman. The great house, or the meeting place, of the kraal is under control of the chief woman but other women cannot enter it.

The practice of *lobola,* or bridewealth, is common among Swazi people, but its role is gradually changing. Traditionally, a groom's family gives cattle to the bride's family at marriage. More educated girls now get higher amounts of lobola, which is more likely to be in the form of cash instead of cattle.

Dress: The majority of the Swazis wear Western-style clothing these days. Traditional clothing materials are animal skins, leather, and cotton. Women make intricately beaded ornaments that they wear on special social occasions. When making public appearances, the king often wears leopard skins and red lourie bird feathers in his hair.

Handicrafts: Most Swazi women produce some craft items as a way to earn extra money. Handicrafts are marketed through various organizations and outlets. Crafts are chiefly pottery making, mohair tapestries, leather work, jewelry, clothing, sculpture, glass, silk-screen painting, and basket weaving. Swedish glassblowers trained Swazis in the ancient craft of glass blowing, and it has since become a major product of Swaziland. Ngwenya Glass, one of the oldest firms in Swaziland, uses exclusively recycled glass.

Housing: Swazis live in round huts placed on the perimeter of common cattle areas. The kraal huts are built from local materials and differ from one region to another. Dried grasses are used in the middle and high ranges while branches and saplings are used in wooded areas. Separate huts for sleeping, cooking, and storing food are placed at specific points around the krall. When a Swazi man marries, he builds his home near his mother's; if he marries more than once, the kraal grows into a little village.

Food: Maize (corn) is the staple food. It is ground into meal which is then cooked into a porridge that is the staple dish for most of the Swazi people. Corn is also eaten roasted or boiled or directly off the cob.

Sports and Recreation: There is very little organized sports activity of any kind. Swimming is popular among schoolchildren who have access to a swimming pool. Traditional music plays an important role in the Swazi social life. Popular instruments are rattles, shields, buckhorn whistles, and long reed flutes.

Tourism: Swaziland offers various tourist attractions such as game reserves and mountain scenery. During the apartheid years in South Africa, visitors coming to South Africa found it easier and better to vacation in Swaziland where racial tensions were not an issue and tourist facilities were readily available. This gave Swaziland's tourism industry a big boost. The Royal Swazi Sun Hotel and Casino is the best-known resort and convention center in the country.

Social Welfare: People generally take care of their elderly and sick at home. Some social service provisions, such as old age, disability, and survivor pensions are provided by the government.

IMPORTANT DATES

400—The Nguni-speaking people begin to move into the Swaziland area.
1750—King Ngwane III leads his people across the Lubombo Mountains from Mozambique to present-day Swaziland.
1828—Zulu warrior Dingaan storms Swaziland with his army.
1845—The Swazi king gives land to the Boers in the eastern Transvaal.
1855—More land is given to the Boers in the northwest Transvaal.
1871—The Anglicans establish a mission.
1875—King Mbandzeni is crowned.
1877—The British annex the Transvaal region to their South African colony.

1878—The British are defeated by the Zulus at the Battle of Isandhlwana.

1881—The British repeal the annexation of Transvaal and recognize Swaziland's independence.

1887—Theophilus Shepstone arrives in Swaziland as a land-claims advisor to the Swazi king; the Berlin Missionary Society members arrive in Swaziland.

1888—King Mbandzeni grants a charter to some five hundred whites, allowing self-government.

1889—Rinderpest attack kills thousands of cattle and wildlife.

1892—The town of Bremersdorp (now called Manzini) is established.

1894—The Swaziland Convention turns the country into a political dependency of Transvaal; Bhunu becomes the monarch under the name of King Ngwane V; rinderpest kills virtually all Swazi livestock; a school for whites is opened at Bremersdorp.

1897—A British head tax forces Africans into wage-earning jobs.

1899—War breaks out between the Boers and the English-speaking whites of South Africa; Boers surrender in 1901.

1902—A peace treaty is signed between the Boers and the British; the British take control of Transvaal; the town of Mbabane is established by the British.

1906—Control of Swaziland is transferred from the governor of Transvaal to the British High Commissioner of South Africa.

1907—Swaziland is partitioned into "native," European, and Crown Land areas.

1913—A Swazi delegation travels to London to regain land given to Europeans and land taken as Crown Land; the Native Recruiting Corporation, an office of the Transvaal Chamber of Mines, opens in Swaziland to hire mine workers for South African mines.

1921—King Sobhuza II is crowned.

1923—Another delegation travels to London to regain Swazi land given to Europeans and land taken as Crown Land.

1925—Dr. David Hynd, a missionary and physician, arrives from Scotland.

1938—Asbestos deposits are discovered in the north at Havelock.

1939—Dr. Mastbaum arrives from Germany; he embarks on a program to spray DDT in huts to eradicate malaria.

1944—Native Administration Proclamation is issued by the British.

1949—The Usutu Pine Forest project starts.

1950—Another Native Administration Proclamation is issued by the British.

1953—King Sobhuza II attends the coronation of Queen Elizabeth II.

1956—Country's first sugar mill becomes operational.

1960—Usutu Pulp Company is established.

1967—General elections are held; a parliament is elected; Swaziland is officially made a British protectorate; Sobhuza II is installed as king; the Sugar Act is passed to regulate sugar production.

1968—Swaziland becomes independent; it also becomes a member of the

United Nations and the Organization of African Unity (OAU).

1972—In country's first general elections, King Sobhuza's political party, the Imbokodvo National Movement, loses several seats in the government.

1973—King Sobhuza repeals the constitution and dissolves parliament, banning all political parties by a royal proclamation.

1974—Mantenga Craft Center opens; a new national currency, the *lilangeni,* is introduced.

1978—A new constitution is proclaimed; the document is never published and all preparations are kept secret; commercial production of iron ore ends at the Ngwenya mine.

1982—King Sobhuza II dies at the age of 83.

1983—15-year-old Crown Prince Makhosetive is formally presented to the Swazi people.

1985—The National Maize Corporation is established.

1986—Prince Makhosetive is crowned as King Mswati III.

1987—King Mswati III dissolves parliament; new elections are held.

1989—The Cadbury Swaziland plant starts manufacturing chocolates; miners stage a strike at the Havelock asbestos mine over low wages.

1993—Parliamentary elections are held.

1994—Swaziland hosts a joint ministerial meeting of the European Union (EU) and African, Caribbean, and Pacific (ACP) states.

1995—A new high school is opened with a special curriculum in electronics and mechanical engineering; a group is formed to write a new constitution; King Mswati III attends the Fiftieth Anniversary celebration of the United Nations in New York.

1996—Barnabas Sibusiso Dlamini is appointed prime minister.

IMPORTANT PEOPLE

James Allison, one of the first Wesleyan missionaries, who came to Swaziland and developed a script based on siSwati language.

Bhunu (–1899), reigned as King Ngwane V for just five years; died at age 23.

Dlamini, a leader of the first Swazi people, known as the bakaMswati and bakaNgwane.

Queen Mother Dzeliwe, King Sobhuza's eldest wife; she sent Crown Prince Makhosetive to England to school, ignoring a great deal of opposition from the *liqoqo* (royal inner council). When she dismissed the entire liqoqo, senior members of the royal house of Dlamini retaliated by removing her from office.

Austin Hleza, one of the best contemporary artists, sculptors, and printmakers; his subjects are everyday scenes from Swazi life.

Dr. David Hynd, a Scottish missionary and medical doctor; he built a hospital at Manzini and trained teachers, nurses, and evangelists; it was through his efforts that leprosy was largely eliminated from Swaziland by 1961.

Queen Mother Labotsibeni Mdluli, acting head of state (1899 to 1921) for her son Bhunu and then for her grandson.

Mbandzeni (–1889), a son of King Mswati I; he was crowned after Ludvonga, King Mswati's chosen heir, died before taking the throne.

Allister Miller, a British journalist who served as advisor to Swazi king Mbandzeni; he was responsible for the Swazi monarchy's loss of a great deal of land.

Mswati II (–1865), king of Swaziland; son of Sobhuza I; considered Swaziland's greatest fighting king; he adopted the practice of "age regiments," known for their military skill and discipline; he introduced Christianity to Swaziland and united many different clans into a nation.

Mswati III (1968–), Makhosetive, a son of Queen Ntombi and King Sobhuza II; chosen to be the king after Sobhuza's death in 1982; took the name of Mswati III when he became king in 1986.

Queen Regent Ntombi, a wife of King Sobhuza II and mother of Mswati III.

Ndvungunya, Swazi king; son of Ngwane III.

Ngwane III, great Swazi king who led his people from Mozambique to the present-day Swaziland.

Andries Potgieter (1800?–1853), a Dutch leader of the Boers who was awarded a large block of land in return for one hundred head of cattle.

Albert C. and Marie-Louise Reck, husband and wife team who came to Swaziland in the mid-1970s and started a major tapestries business with local weavers.

Ted Reilly, rancher and wildlife conservationist who created and nurtured the Mkhaya Nature Reserve and Mlilwane Wildlife Sanctuary.

Sir Theophilus Shepstone (1817–1893), the most trusted white (British) advisor to Swazi and other African kings.

Theophilus Shepstone, son of Sir Theophilus Shepstone, land-claims advisor to the King Mbandzeni; came to Swaziland in 1887.

Sobhuza I (? –1836), Swazi king; son of Ndvungunya.

Sobhuza II (1899–1982), one of the longest ruling kings in the world; reigned from 1921 to 1982; his reign is considered a remarkable blend of tradition and adaptation of modern life.

Jennie Thorn, encourages crafts among rural women; established Tishweshwe and Gone Rural craft business; her work specializes in pottery and products made from lutindzi, a local grass.

Pauline Woodall, created the nonprofit Mantenga Craft Center, which encourages women to be self-sufficient by creating and selling craft items.

Compiled by Chandrika Kaul, Ph.D.

INDEX

Page numbers that appear in **boldface type** indicate illustrations

About the Authors

Ettagale Blauer has been writing about Africa for young adult readers for twenty years. She has written three books for one series on South Africa, Portugal, and Bangladesh, in collaboration with Jason Lauré. Their book on Bangladesh was nominated for the National Book Award. In the Enchantment of the World series, she has written *Tanzania* and *Mozambique* in collaboration with Jason Lauré.

Ms. Blauer has traveled widely in Africa, including a year in South Africa and a three-month-long overland trip from Morocco to Kenya. She has visited many diamond and gold mines during her reserach and says she knows the continent "from beneath the ground and up."

Born in New York City, Ms. Blauer was graduated from Hunter College with a degree in creative writing. Ms. Blauer also is well known in the field of jewelry writing and is the author of *Contemporary American Jewelry Design.*

Jason Lauré was born in Chehalis, Washington, and lived in California before joining the United States Army and serving in France. He attended Columbia University and worked for *The New York Times.* He traveled to San Francisco and became a photographer during the turbulent 1960s. Mr. Lauré recorded those events before setting out on the first of many trips to Africa.

Mr. Lauré covers the political life of that continent and also has made a number of expeditions across the Sahara. He has written about, and photographed in, forty countries in Africa.

In the Enchantment of the World series, Mr. Lauré has written books on Zimbabwe, Bangladesh, Angola, Zambia, Namibia, and Botswana, and has collaborated on *Tanzania* and *Mozambique* with Ettagale Blauer.

Mr. Lauré is married to Marisia Lauré, a translator. Based in New York, he spends half of each year in Africa. They have a daughter, Mirella.